YOUR MIND THE MAGICIAN

As if by Magic, the Pictures You Choose and Hold in Front of Your Creative Mechanism Determine the Results You Get. Do Your Pictures Include Their Happening Now?

IF NOT NOW, WHEN?

Allen M. Rosenthal

DEVORSS Publications

Library of Congress Card Catalog Number: 90-82481
ISBN: 0-87516-619-9
Second Printing, 1993

Artwork by Carol Hoss
Cover Design by Gary Peattie

DeVorss & Company, Publisher
P.O. Box 550
Marina del Rey, CA 90294

Printed in the United States of America

Contents

List of Illustrations

Preface

According to the *American Heritage Dictionary*, the word *magic* refers to the creation of supernatural results. In other words, a result is "magical" when the "how" of its creation is beyond our conscious understanding and expectation. By the time you get very far into this book you'll see the extraordinary and "supernatural" role your mind plays, as if by magic, in creating the things you point it at every day.

In 1983 when I started writing this book, and lecturing about the principles it contains, my purpose was as follows:

1. that the success I have with it will be a demonstration of the power of the Creative Mechanism about which I write and speak;
2. that others will be inspired enough by that to give up their negative perspectives and focus on what they WANT, trusting themselves to create it; and
3. that enough people will be so inspired, that the world as a whole will subscribe to, and thereby realize, a vision of all peoples living truly in abundance, peace and harmony, with freedom, dignity and respect for themselves, each other and their environment.

Out of my commitment to these principles, in 1985 I began participating in citizen diplomacy trips to the Soviet Union and East Germany. On these trips I met and was inspired by many wonderful people. I find it interesting to notice what has now transpired in the world out of so many people from the United States and the East-bloc countries having the courage to take a stand for the VISION of a peaceful, friendly world. I wrote in 1985 that the critical mass of such people had in fact been achieved. Amen and Hallelujah!

The human mind contains one of the most effective tools for guiding human creativity conceivable. And it doesn't need to be "fixed." We need simply to be more *aware* of its existence and what it can do. We then can more consciously choose to use it, just the way we choose to use hammers on nails and screwdrivers on screws.

The problem is that this creative machinery is so good at what it does, at the automatic reflex level, we don't even notice that it exists. This book is intended to give you an *awareness* of your inherent creative machinery and thereby empower you to use it more consciously, and in a more *positive* direction.

Maxwell Maltz, in his profound *Psycho Cybernetics,* alternately referred to this human creative machinery as the "Success Mechanism" and "Creative Mechanism." I like the term "Creative Mechanism," because the composite definition* of those two words translates into a very apt description of what that machinery is and how it works automatically to create whatever we point it at. That definition is:

THE PRIMARY AND NOVEL INSTRUMENT BY WHICH THINGS WE HAVE NOT YET SEEN OR EXPERIENCED ARE BROUGHT INTO BEING THROUGH THE FORMATION OF MENTAL IMAGES.

*The composite definition of *Creative Mechanism* is developed as follows:

Creative is defined as: "Characterized by originality; imaginative."

Mechanism is defined as: "An instrument or process by which something is done or comes into being."

The key words in *creative* are "originality" and "imaginative." *Originality* means "primary or novel" and *imaginative* means "the process or power of forming a mental image of something that is not or has not been seen or experienced."

The most unique characteristic of the human mind is its ability to imagine. *Imagination* is defined as "the power to form mental images of things we have not yet seen or experienced." Even Albert Einstein recognized the importance of imagination when he said:

> *When I examine myself and my methods of thought I come to the conclusion that the gift of fantasy has meant more to me than my talent for absorbing positive knowledge.*

It is this inherent ability to IMAGINE, and the power to then CHOOSE to HAVE, things we have not yet seen or experienced that works the "magic" in our lives. Charles Garfield, in his book *Peak Performers,* reported that *every* peak performer he studied maintained that:

> *The potential for major increases in achievement and self-development exists in everyone, and . . . the starting point is an internal decision to excel.*

I guarantee that if you play the games and do the processes suggested in this book, you'll have an experience of the magical power of your Creative Mechanism.

Once you "taste" its existence, you'll start noticing how much of your daily life it's already handling for you. The more you notice it, the more you'll trust it. The more you trust it, the more you'll consciously choose to use it, and the more spectacular will be the results you achieve with it. Then you'll trust it all the more.

There will be nothing to "figure out" and little or no pain or struggle in the process. There will be the feeling of "flow," like water flowing downhill, effortlessly being true to its own essential, fluid nature—flowing *around* the obstacles in its path. There'll be nothing to "fix," "handle," "heal," "change," "break through," or get "free" from, in the traditional sense. And life and the world will turn out more the way you WANT it to. And even more importantly, whether it turns out or not won't be as significant to you. And you'll have a whole lot more fun participating in the process.

The mind is probably even more powerful than what we have the courage at this time to imagine. However, as with the discovery of the wheel, its profundity is probably in its obvious simplicity, which we all take for granted.

I invite you to compare the model of the mind reflected in these pages with your own life's experience and let your own intuition tell you whether or not it has the ring of truth. If it does, I want you to use it to create the world we all want. I have found the increased awareness of the magical nature of my Creative Mechanism very empowering in expanding my own participation and fulfillment in life. I recommend it to you.

But be aware, however, that your mind is *not* who you are. Your mind is something very valuable that *you have*. You can use it more consciously and effectively, if you'll just get to know it better.

I must acknowledge that I have not yet created everything I want in my life with this tool. The old saw, that we tend to teach what we need to learn, seems to be very accurate in my case. However, the surrender, fulfillment and joy in my life have expanded every time I work on, or talk about, what's in this book. And I keep getting glowing responses to it from people who read it. So, I've decided that I don't have to wait until I have created all the things I want through the use of these principles before formally publishing them.

So, let's begin.

Acknowledgments

FIRST OF ALL, I must thank my mother, father, sister, her husband, my niece and nephew, who have demonstrated beyond doubt that they love me, no matter what.

In chronological order of my contact with them, I also want to specifically acknowledge those people whose participation in the world has inspired me to greater participation:

The late Maxwell Maltz, M.D., for his book, *Psycho Cybernetics,* which I view as an observation as profound as the discovery of the wheel; John Wooden (and the UCLA Basketball Teams of 1964–1976) for their demonstration of the incredible success achievable through letting go of "win/lose" and committing to participation to the fullest; Werner Erhard of the "est" Training for giving me a heightened experience of my "mind" and for the insightful use of definitions; the late Brandon St. John, Marilyn Atteberry and Noel Roth of the "Sage Experience," from whose dynamic example I learned to trust myself; Ken Minyard and Bob Arthur of the "Ken and Bob Show" on KABC Radio in Los Angeles, for their pioneering of the "positive's where it's at" with their "EGBOK" acronym for "EVERYTHING'S GONNA BE OKAY"; Robert Fritz of DMA, Inc., for so beautifully expressing the simplicity and power of "CHOICE"; Barbara Marx Hubbard and her "Campaign for a Positive Future," and Rama Vernon and Ed and Linda Johnson and the Center for Soviet-American Dialogue, who gave me the opportunity and inspiration to participate in making the principles in this book a reality at world level; Ram Dass, for setting such a beautiful example of self-consciousness and the "spiritual journey"—I cannot count the number of times I've gotten recentered by listening to tapes of his lectures; and the late Alan Watts, for so beautifully expressing the "oneness" of it all.

I also want to acknowledge people like Mikhail Gorbachev (who, in my view, will go down in history as one of the most courageous men of all time); Drs. Bernard Lown and Evgeni Chazov and International Physicians for Prevention of Nuclear War; Dr. Helen Caldicott and Pauline and Dr. Richard Saxon and the Physicians for Social Responsibility; Ted Turner and his Goodwill Games and Better World Society; John Denver and the Windstar Foundation; Dennis Weaver and wife, Gerri, and Valerie Harper and Love Is Feeding Everyone; Jerry Jampolsky and Diane Cirincione and Children as Teachers of Peace; Rev. Peggy Bassett of the Huntington Beach Church of Religious Science; Hans-Georg Pape and the Dixieland Allstars of East Berlin; and John Konstanturos and Diane Harber, then of the Los Angeles Police Department, and the Committee on Transformation of Organizations—all of whom by their willingness to participate in, and stand up *in public* for, the peaceful, positive, abundant world we all want, have set magnificent examples and inspired the rest of us. And I know there are many others, whose names I can't think of right now. But they know they have done their part.

Thank you, all. I stand on your shoulders.

I also want to thank the many people who've allowed me to share my thoughts with them and discover myself in that process. It seems to me that in giving me the opportunity to express myself to them, those people have really assisted me to discover myself. To them I say Thank You for that gift! They include all my schoolmates (especially brothers Bob and Larry Bretter), Jeannie Presser, Gail Ellen, June Shute, Joy Ballin, Anne Redstone, Helen Moran, Linda Stephens, Madeleine Schwab and Christine Maginn.

Special thanks go to Gloria Sherwood and Lauren Gold who

were there at, and supported me through, my first high school lecture. Special thanks also go to Gary Leversee, Lynn Tharsing, Rosalyn Kalmar, John Holmdahl, Marcia Seligson, Beverly Livingston, Nancy Fredericks, and JacQuaeline for their suggestions, support, and encouragement in getting this book to completion and publication.

I would be remiss if I did not also acknowledge the opportunity to play my banjo to Michael Elley's music in the USSR and East Germany. Michael's music inspired me to levels of participation I never dreamed possible for a little 'ole self-taught ukelele player like myself.

I also want to acknowledge and thank the *American Heritage Dictionary*. The quoted definitions of specific individual words are from the *American Heritage Dictionary*, unless otherwise noted. The "composite" definitions are, for the most part, a combination of the dictionary definitions of the key words within the original dictionary definitions.

And last but not least, my eternal gratitude goes to Arthur Vergara of DeVorss & Company for his insightful editorial suggestions and support.

If I overlooked anyone, please let me know and forgive me.

1

I Know Who You Are

We're all functionally the same—you are me and I am you. And who we are is "okay."

THE FIRST thing we need to establish is the fact that we're all functionally the same.

If you think about it for a moment, you'll see that it would be unrealistic to expect otherwise. Are we not all a part of the same species? Do we not all have the same basic biological and psychological equipment?

Did we not all have the same basic needs as children? Did we not all get told to behave like an "adult," whatever that is? Did we not all copy or resist copying some of our parents' ways of being? Have we not all struggled to be somebody "special" and to be acknowledged as "okay"?

Have we not all at some time or another thought we were supposed to be like somebody else?

Just as the essential characteristics of all snowflakes are the same, even though no two of them have exactly the same crystal structure, so it is throughout nature. Why should our species be any different? The truth is that we've all really started with the same basic machinery and gone through the same kinds of experiences.

Even though no two of us will have had the exact same experiences, in exactly the same order and timing, the essential characteristics of what it is to be a human being must be the same for all of us.

So, if I know myself (i.e. how I function), then I must also know you. And, equally, you know me.

Anyway, what I want you to imagine right now is that you've told me who you are, what your life's struggles have been and what it is you really WANT to have in your life. Imagine that there's somebody out there named Allen Rosenthal who really knows how all that feels.

If there's anything that you feel about yourself right now that you think I don't know, just notice what that is, and know that I know how that feels, too. Know that you are me, and I am you—and that you're "OKAY," just the way you are—RIGHT NOW. AND I'M GOING TO PROVE IT TO YOU IN THIS BOOK! (There's nothing in you that needs "fixing." You just have to better understand who you really are and practice being more conscious of where you're pointing that.)

Now that you know you're okay with ME, just the way you are, we'll create you being okay with YOU that way, too.

2

The Marvelous Guidance System You Already Have

There exists in each of us a computer-like (''cybernetic'') guidance system (''Creative Mechanism'') that guides us through the ''doingness'' of everything we do.

HAVE YOU ever noticed how the most obvious aspects of things escape your awareness?

A few years ago, at a time when I was particularly agonizing over some unsuccessful aspects of my life, it occurred to me that if I examined what I had already accomplished, I might discover some techniques I could use to good advantage in my present pursuits. In answer to that inquiry, some hitherto unconscious, but obvious, aspects of human creativity came to my awareness.

To my amazement, what I saw was that the ''doingness'' of all human activity occurs not at conscious or rational level, but at reflex level. (The term *doingness* is used here to refer to the specific behavioral inputs or elements that produce a particular intended circumstantial result or output, in a pure cause-and-effect sense.) The specific individual elements that make up all human activity are subject to the direction of a cybernetic-like guidance system (what Maxwell Maltz very accurately called the ''Creative Mechanism'').

For example, if you've turned one of the pages of this book, you've used your Creative Mechanism. Consider for a moment what the ''doingness'' was in turning the page. The ''doingness'' involved in turning the page was your physically locating and isolating the particular page, grasping that page between the thumb and forefinger of your right hand, and moving your hand in a way that moved the page to its new position. You probably then held that page down with the fingers of your left hand, while sliding your right hand back to its original position.

Do you know specifically which muscles you triggered into flexing, to what degree, or in what order, in accomplishing that result? Were you "conscious" or "aware" of figuring out and premeditating that sequence? Of course you were not.

Of what were you "conscious"? Look back at the experience. Probably the only thing you can remember "doing" was that at some point in time you made a CHOICE as to what it was you wanted to accomplish—i.e. seeing the next page. Then, you let it happen. There was a lot going on, however, at reflex level (in your Creative Mechanism) that got the job done. Given the vision of what you had just CHOSEN as your intended result, *something* determined and produced the specific contractions in just the right muscles, and in just the right magnitude and order, that were required to produce the chosen result.

Consider how you would go about getting out of the chair in which you're now sitting. You would not be conscious of the individual muscles you'd use, or in what order you'd use them. You would simply envision (i.e. picture in your mind) yourself getting up, or maybe see yourself in the next room, and then notice yourself doing whatever it takes to accomplish that result.

One of my favorite examples of the existence and effectiveness of this wonderful Creative Mechanism in action is an infant learning to walk. Remember how this usually takes place before the infant has learned to talk. All it has in the way of instruction is about a year's experience of observing other human beings walking. Once an infant learns to stand and balance itself long enough to lift a foot off the floor, it discovers that it falls over backwards unless it first leans forward a little before stepping.

Did you ever balance a baseball bat, or some other elongated object, like a broomstick, vertically on end in the palm of your hand? That little game demonstrates the principle of physics involved in walking. You must keep moving the point of support of the object under its center of gravity, or the object will fall over. In balancing a bat, you literally keep moving the point where your hand touches the bat under where the rest of the bat was about to fall, so as to keep the bat in balance.

Walking literally consists of deliberately tilting your body's center of gravity out of balance in the direction of the intended step, and then moving your foot (the point of support) under where you just put your center of gravity. Without the lean of your body, you'd fall over backwards. Without the step, your body would fall on its face. (See Figure 1, p. 7.)

And please notice that when you walk, this whole process takes place at reflex level, once you CHOOSE your destination. What a marvelous computer-like ("cybernetic") guidance system must be present in each of us that, at the age of approximately one year, we can so monitor and refine our physical experience and learn to walk!

And remember how when an infant first discovers the necessity to lean forward, it leans a little too far at first and has to almost run to have its feet catch up with its body. Very quickly, however, its guidance system (its Creative Mechanism) refines its responses into just the right combination of leaning and stepping. Imagine how well developed and effective the Creative Mechanisms of Olympic and professional athletes and concert musicians must be for them to achieve the performances they achieve. They cannot "think" their way through the "doingness" of those results.

Start noticing, right now, how much of the detail or "doingness" of your own daily life is being handled at reflex level by your own amazing Creative Mechanism. I think you'll be astonished to see just how much actually takes place at that level.

An interesting and very accurate metaphor for human behavior to note here is that:

MOVING TO ANY NEW PLACE IN LIFE LITERALLY INVOLVES DELIBERATELY PUTTING ONE'S SELF *OUT OF BALANCE* IN THE DIRECTION OF THE INTENDED DESTINATION, AND *THEN* TRUSTING YOUR CREATIVE MECHANISM TO CREATE THE NECESSARY POINTS OF SUPPORT.

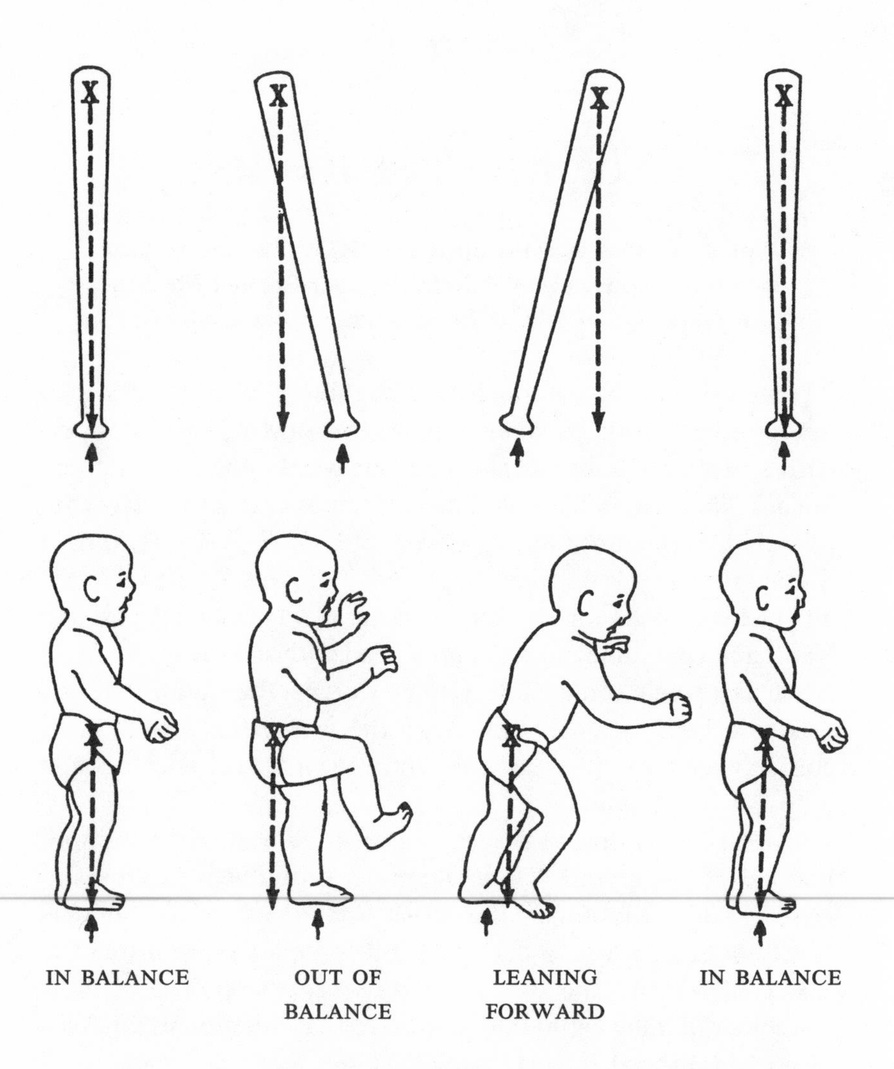

Figure 1. The Amazing Phenomenon of Walking

3

Cybernetics at Its Best

You don't have to consciously see "HOW" to create what you want in advance of choosing it. Your Creative Mechanism takes care of that at the automatic reflex level.

THE ESSENCE of computerized machinery is that, once programmed for a particular result, the control function is performed automatically. That's what the word *cybernetic* literally means. The human Creative Mechanism operates that way too.

I vividly remember, as a gymnast at UCLA, learning to do a double somersault on the trampoline. The first few times in the air, I tried to deliberately "think" what it was I was supposed to "do" and each time landed on my head without having made so much as a single somersault. (Don't worry—the trampoline bed was soft, and my head was none the worse for wear.) But I couldn't seem to think fast enough to "think" my way through a double somersault.

Eventually, almost in desperation, I stood next to the trampoline and said to myself: "Wait a minute. A double is just two singles. I've done thousands of singles. What would it look and feel like to hold a tuck long enough for it to be a *double* instead of just a single?" To this day, some forty years later, I can vividly remember literally getting the answer to that question in the form of a picture that I intently visualized and mentally rehearsed. I then got back on the trampoline and noticed myself easily doing a double somersault without having done anything more than give myself a clear mental picture of what it was I wanted to accomplish, rehearsing the experience of it in my mind a few times.

Looking back at that experience, it is clear to me now that there was some kind of internal, automatic guidance system operating for me, once I had CHOSEN and mentally rehearsed a *present* experience of the result I wanted to create.

When my 6-year-old niece first tried to ride a two-wheel bicycle, she had great difficulty. When she finally got it, I asked her what she'd done between my visits that had enabled her to learn bicycle riding. Her quick reply was, "I watched Eddie and practiced a lot." Eddie was the boy next door, who already knew how to ride a two-wheeler. What an amazing phenomenon! This 43-pound 6-year-old learned to ride a two-wheeler by imitating the boy next door. As a matter of fact, isn't that how you did it too? When I thought about it, I realized that I learned to be an expert skier the same way—constantly watching what the good skiers were doing, and then practicing or mentally rehearsing the "imitation" of that. I suggest that's how we learned everything we now know how to do.

Some years ago, I saw some film on television of a former pro-basketball great with the San Francisco Warriors, named Rick Barry, shooting and making 25 free throws in a row! The camera then moved to a short, pudgy, middle-aged man standing at a free-throw line. This man was wearing a blindfold, but proceeded to make 22 out of 25 free-throw attempts without ever taking the blindfold off. Talk about "That's Incredible!" I remember thinking, at the time, that what these guys did was so far beyond any ability I might have, that they must've come from another planet.

Now that I've identified and "tasted" the existence of my *own* Creative Mechanism, I know that these gentlemen were born with no more physical equipment than I have. They just focused theirs on basketball shooting and practiced enough to achieve the high level of results they wanted.

If you want to have some fun and experience or "taste" your own Creative Mechanism in action, play the following game: Throw candies or paper clips, or some such objects, into a large rolled-down paper bag, or a waste basket, from four or five feet away. In other words, use the paper bag or waste basket as something like a basketball basket (we'll call that the "basket"), and then throw things into it from no more than five foot lengths away.

So that you can clearly see the difference when you practice some "technique," throw first, just the way you would've thrown before reading this book. Count how many objects you actually get into the basket out of the total you throw, doing it that way.

Then, make the same throws again, but this time CHOOSING, VISUALIZING and REHEARSING *before* EACH THROW a picture of the object going into and hitting the bottom of the basket. Do that just the way I imagined myself accomplishing a double somersault, before I actually accomplished it. See the object in the basket. Imagine the "thump" or "plop" you'd hear when an object of that type hits the bottom of the basket. Let go of any concern for "how" to do it. Just throw, trusting your Creative Mechanism to take care of guiding your hand, just the way you trust your hand to get food from your plate to your mouth when you eat. Say to yourself as you throw, "IN THE BASKET."

After each throw, notice and correlate the state of mind you had (i.e. the picture or thought you had of the result you expected just as you threw) with the actual result you got. Notice whether you were "in your hand," thinking about how difficult it would be, or trying to consciously tell your hand "how" to throw, or whether you were focused on the successful result and "trusting" your Creative Mechanism to produce it.

Now, do the same process, VISUALIZING and REHEARSING before each throw, as before, but closing your eyes just at the beginning and during each throw, still trusting your Creative Mechanism to take care of the "how." My experience is that I'm MORE accurate with my eyes closed than with them open. I get a clear sense that, with my eyes closed, I'm less distracted by thoughts of how difficult it looks. (As we'll see in Ch. 12, thinking about what can go wrong very often is the very thing that keeps us from achieving the results we want.) I have a friend who literally got a hole-in-one, teeing off with his eyes closed, as I'd suggested.

Experiment with seeing the whole target, instead of just the bull's-eye. In other words, instead of focusing on the small bull's-eye-like basket, imagine the basket being the center of something much LARGER, like a garbage can.

Stretch your perspective by moving 50 percent or more farther away from the basket, and notice the effect that has on your mind's expectations about your accuracy. After a few throws from that distance, move back to the original distance and notice how much easier it feels, and how your accuracy improves.

Now, say out loud, "I'M A GOOD BOY/GIRL," just before each throw, and notice what happens.

Take a deep breath and let it out with a "whoosh" before each throw, thinking "RELAX." You might even visualize the word *RELAX* printed across the basket. An important ingredient, through all these experiments, is to RELAX your self-consciousness and concern about the "HOW." Focus your attention and intention on the basket and the successful result you want.

If you play the games outlined above, you'll get a first-hand "taste" of your Creative Mechanism in action, just as you "tasted" what bicycle riding was that first moment you realized you'd actually ridden a bicycle. Figuratively and literally, just "close your eyes" to all the things that could go wrong, and stay focused on the desired result. You'll see unmistakably how easily your Creative Mechanism can be used, and how accurate it can actually be, when you get the rational "thinking" out of the "doingness" and instead trust the magician in your mind.

Those of you who have seen firewalking have probably heard about how important not looking at the hot coals is to successful firewalking. The mind has been programmed to equate hot coals with burns, and guess what you get if you look down and see what it is you're walking on.

I find dart-throwing games a much easier way to experience the power of my Creative Mechanism. I use my effectiveness at throwing games as a model for the most effective way to operate in creating the other things in my life.

I keep a felt target board and some velcro-wrapped pingpong-ball-like darts at home and in my office with which to play periodically to remind myself of the existence of my automatic Creative Mechanism. Or I just throw paper clips into a cookie can. I recommend that you do the same. Use it as an "anchor" or "conditioned response" to remind yourself of the existence of your very own magical Creative Mechanism and how effective it can be when you TRUST IT.

So, modeled after successful basket-shooting or dart-throwing, here's a game plan for creating results in your life:

1. **CHOOSE** a good general picture of the RESULT you WANT.
2. **LET GO** of needing to "pin-point" the bull's eye and **FOCUS** on the LARGER picture you want to create.
3. **REHEARSE** in your mind's eye, with all of your senses—sight, feeling, sound and smell—actually experiencing the successful result you want.
4. **RELAX**—take the significance out of the result, and have it be the experience of "game" and "fun."
5. **TRUST** your Creative Mechanism to produce the "how" and the actual "doingness" at automatic reflex level.
6. **VISUALIZE** only the positive result you want.
7. **MOVE** in the direction of the desired result without having to first see the "perfect" method for getting all the way there. In other words, be willing to "trial-and-error" your way there.
8. **STRETCH** your perspective from time to time about what is possible.

9. **AFFIRM** your own okayness and worthiness to have the successful result by saying, "I AM A GOOD BOY/GIRL."

From the foregoing, I think it is evident that the "HOW" of whatever we want to create is produced and controlled by our own Creative Mechanism at the automatic reflex level. Therefore, we need not be so limited or careful in the kinds of things we CHOOSE to create in our lives or the world.

Remember the old adage: "The difficult we do right now, the impossible may take a little while." I think the guy who said that knew something very important. The easy stuff—like turning pages or getting out of chairs—will come right away. A truly peaceful and harmonious world may take a little longer. The point is, however, that if our Creative Mechanisms take care of creating the "doingness," you and I can probably be a whole lot more courageous than we've been up to now in the choices we make about what we want to create.

4

It's Already "On"

You're born with your Creative Mechanism in the "ON" position, and it can't be turned off. You'd better pay more attention to where you're pointing it.

BECAUSE OF my belief in the analogy between the mind and computers, I used to think that the use of my Creative Mechanism involved two steps: first, CHOOSING the vision of what I WANTED, and second, pushing the return or "go" key to put it all in motion. However, when I first started writing this book and looked more closely at the second step, I couldn't identify or isolate anything in my experience that would qualify as pushing any kind of return or "go" key. I was momentarily baffled, since I was certain that something had to initiate the "doingness" for any results to be produced. I actually gave up the idea of writing this book, and was walking away from my desk, when my Creative Mechanism gave me the answer.

That little voice in the back of my head whispered in my ear that the reason I couldn't remember ever turning anything "ON" was that MY CREATIVE MECHANISM WAS ALREADY "ON." In fact, IT'S *ALWAYS* "ON." We're all born with it already "ON." And we can't ever shut it off. How else could infants learn to walk and talk?

What a beautiful "AHA!"

ALL MY LIFE, I'D BEEN TRYING TO FIGURE OUT HOW TO TURN MY CREATIVITY "ON," AND THE DARN THING WAS "ON" ALL THE TIME! (Sound familiar?)

Your Creative Mechanism is constantly determining and producing visible behavior (and, for all I know, some not-so-visible behavior like radio or other waves or impulses), according to what it's being told by the pictures you CHOOSE and HOLD of the result you WANT and EXPECT to happen. It's there, functioning *at all times*, as any self-respecting cybernetic mechanism would function. It's your nervous and guidance system, monitoring your current circumstances, scanning your past experience (which includes, by the way, what you've assimilated from others), and selecting and producing the detailed behavior within your current ability and experience that's most consistent with those circumstances and the result you've CHOSEN and EXPECT.

It is therefore apparent that, from moment to moment, the PICTURES you've CHOSEN and are HOLDING of what you expect to happen are critical to the results you can expect to accomplish.

Consider right now how nonchalant and unconscious you've probably been with respect to how focused your Creative Mechanism is. I daresay most of us are not very conscious of the existence of this mechanism, let alone where we're pointing it.

Can you really afford to so ignore such an incredible device? What would you lose if you reconnected with its creative potential? If you're anything like me, you'd be noticing right now that you'd not have so much to complain about. In fact, you'd have to give up a lot of the "I can't," "unworthy," and "victim" pictures under which you've been operating, and take responsibility for the rest of your life. (By the way, as we'll see in Ch. 18—"Celebrate Your 'Response-Ability' Now"—that's a lot easier to do than you think.)

The Creative Mechanism literally operates like a magical garden hose that can't be shut off. Whatever receives the nourishing water from this magical hose will grow and expand. If the way to point the hose is simply to CHOOSE and ENVISION what you WANT, it behooves you to be more conscious, from moment to moment, of what PICTURES you've CHOSEN and EXPECT to happen.

At what are you pointing your "hose" right now?

Are you negatively oriented, always pointing it behind you at what you think you have to fix or avoid from your past?

Maybe you don't even know the hose is there at all (i.e. you're not paying any mind to what you want), and the hose is flailing about as hoses do when they're ignored without being shut off. You can't expect your garden to grow in any meaningful way using that technique.

Or are you deliberately pointing it out in front of you at what you really WANT? In other words, are you holding positive thoughts? (See Figure 2.)

The dictionary definitions of the key words *HOLD, PICTURE, WANT* and *EXPECT* give us some help with this phenomenon.

The definition of *HOLD* is "to keep in one's mind or heart, believe, and affirm." *PICTURE* is defined as "the visual representation or image that typifies or embodies an emotion, state of mind, or mood; the chief circumstances of a situation." *WANT* is defined as "to seek with intent to capture." *EXPECT* is defined as "to look forward to the probable occurrence of, to consider as reasonable and due." The composite definition of *reasonable* and *due* is "to consider fitting and appropriate and not excessive or extreme."

Putting all these definitions together, we get a composite description of a technique for pointing your Creative Mechanism:

FROM MOMENT TO MOMENT, KEEP IN YOUR MIND AND HEART, BELIEVE, REGARD, AFFIRM, AND LOOK FORWARD TO THE PROBABLE OCCURRENCE OF, THE CHIEF CIRCUMSTANCES OF THE RESULTS YOU WANT AND EXPECT TO HAPPEN, CONSIDERING THEM AS FITTING AND APPROPRIATE FOR YOURSELF.

Figure 2. Where Are You Pointing Your Hose?

This does not mean pressing to produce the result. It means simply to notice as often as you can where you're pointing your Creative Mechanism, by literally asking yourself the question:

"WHAT PICTURE AM I HOLDING RIGHT NOW OF WHAT I EXPECT TO HAPPEN?"

If the answer you get isn't the one you WANT, CHOOSE and refocus on the one you WANT, and relax, trusting the Creative Mechanism to go to work and produce the behavior and circumstances that are required and appropriate for creating that result. Do that just the way you'd trust it to move your feet when you walk or your mouth when you talk.

If you're thinking to yourself right now, "It can't be that simple," I want you to pat yourself on the top of your head with your right hand. Notice how little mental effort that took, and how automatically produced your hand movements were. Now, just imagine yourself patting yourself on the head that way, but without actually doing it. What is the difference in thought process between having the actual result right now and just imagining it? (Play with that one for a little while. I'll give you the answer at the end of this chapter.)

For a graphic example of this kind of mental control over physical results, the next time you're relieving yourself, notice the mental process you go through in starting and stopping that flow. The mental maneuver involved in making things like that happen is very subtle, but profoundly effective in terms of creating results. I submit that we can use the way we learn to pat ourselves on the head, or be toilet trained, as models for creating any other result we want in our lives.

I recently worked on a very important real estate transaction involving voluminous paperwork and the construction and leasing to my client, on a build-to-suit basis, of a 60,000-square-foot office building worth many millions of dollars. I noticed I was experiencing head and back pains while agonizing over the difficulty I "expected" to have in documenting this transaction.

I noticed that what I was holding in front of my Creative Mechanism was a "horror story" of what I speculated could go wrong with the deal—an occupational disease suffered by many lawyers.

I acknowledged what I saw I'd been doing, and said to myself, "I CHOOSE to have this be easy and turn out successfully." I conjured up in my mind (and this seemed to be an important step) an imaginary picture of the completed building and my client walking in its front door, and I rehearsed that the way I'd rehearsed the double somersault.

The physical and mental pain went away immediately. Within minutes I received telephone calls from other attorneys in the transaction that removed some of the main obstacles to the deal going through. And almost in the same breath, I had the inspiration I needed as to how to structure the rest of the transaction in order to close it. The closing came quickly, easily and painlessly. CHOOSING and REHEARSING a picture of the successful result enabled me to relax and let the positive scenario come forth.

Part and parcel of empowering the Creative Mechanism is the letting go of the significance of the result, and not worrying about HOW you're going to go about creating it. You must trust your Creative Mechanism to take care of the details. If you threw the darts or candies as I suggested in Chapter 3, you should have experienced how much more accurate your results were when you got really FOCUSED on the result, RELAXED and literally "closed your eyes" to how difficult it looked.

Imagine what it would be like to operate in your daily life, at every moment focused on the positive results you want, operating from a state of total and complete relaxation and trust in yourself and your Creative Mechanism. If you can do it throwing darts or candies, putting one foot in front of the other without falling down, patting your head, or relieving yourself, you can do it in every other aspect of your life. Just ask your Creative Mechanism to tell you what that would look and feel like, and CHOOSE, CONTEMPLATE and REHEARSE it.

Play with that thought. You'll find it very worthwhile to conjure up a picture of yourself operating that way on a consistent, daily—yes, even moment-to-moment—basis.

(If you haven't guessed it by now, the only difference between an imagined experience and one that is actually happening is that the picture you've given your Creative Mechanism in the latter case includes the experience of it happening NOW. More about that later in Ch. 8—" 'Rev' Your Engine.")

5

"Cause and Effect" in Reverse

We've been using the law of "Cause and Effect" backwards. In human creativity, the visualization of the desired "output" comes before, and is what produces, the necessary "input."

WHEN IT comes to the human experience of creating results, one of the most obvious, but usually ignored, principles operating in our universe is the law of "cause and effect." It occurred to me one day that for each of the results I've successfully achieved, there were specific causes or things that I'd done that produced them. However, in studying the creative process involved in those experiences, I noticed a trap in traditional "cause and effect" thinking.

Newton's Third Law of Motion is a beautiful and eloquent statement of the "cause and effect" principle: **For every action there is an equal and opposite reaction** (or, **for every input, there is an equal and opposite output**). In my experience, this is absolutely accurate.

It is beautifully demonstrated by the device holding five identical steel balls suspended next to each other in a row so that they bang into each other in pendulum fashion. The reaction (the "Output Group") you get from lifting and letting one, two, three or four of those balls (the "Input Group") impact, in pendulum fashion, the remaining stationary four, three, two or one ball(s) vividly demonstrates the cause-equals-effect principle. (See Figure 3.) The Output Group will always contain the same number of balls that were in the Input Group, even if there were not that

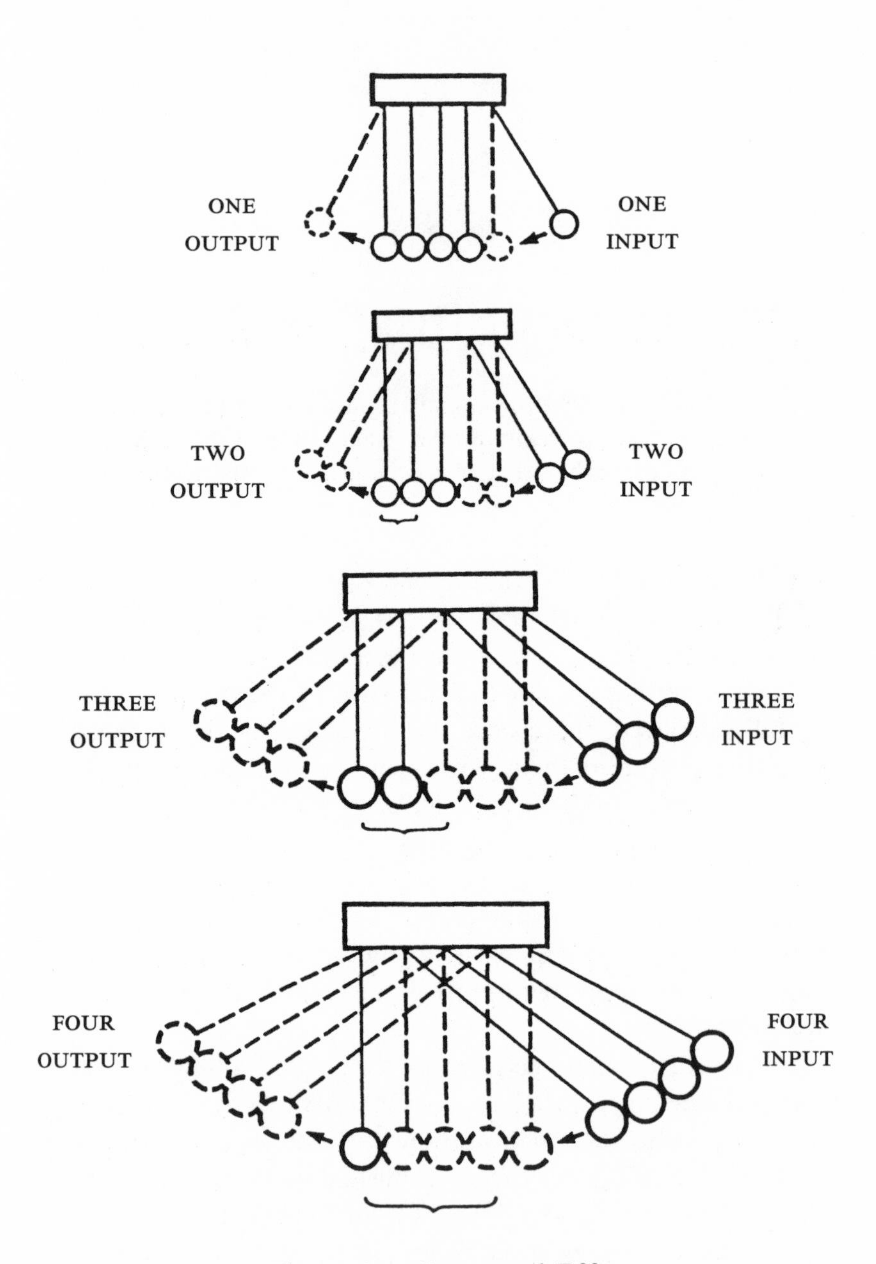

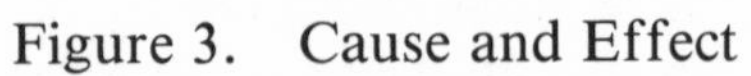

Figure 3. Cause and Effect

many balls left in the stationary group before impact. The necessary number of balls will always be borrowed from the Input Group and go with the Output Group, so that output equals input.

The assumption we've all been making seems to be that, because there is obviously a direct, causal relationship between input and output, all you have to do to successfully create any desired result is determine and create the "right input." Much effort and rational thought is traditionally given to "figuring out" and working on creating the "right input."

However, as we've seen in Chapters 2, 3 and 4, the source of the "right input" is the visualization and rehearsal of the existence of the result—i.e. the OUTPUT. The determination and production of the appropriate "doingness"—the "input"—takes place most effectively at reflex or automatic levels once there is clarity and CHOICE as to the OUTPUT.

If you are spending time and energy trying to figure out the equal and opposite input to what it is you want to create, you must logically have concluded that your inherent creative machinery will not handle that function at reflex level. If that's the instruction you're giving your Creative Mechanism, it will literally be deactivated, and you'll find yourself efforting and struggling to "figure out" and create "inputs," but without any ultimate results. Your life will look like you're doing all the right things, because you'll be busy creating all kinds of "inputs." But you won't be having the bottom-line results you want unless you start focusing on and envisioning that result as a present reality.

If you can give first priority to CHOOSING and having clarity about the result you want to create (the "effect"), trusting your Creative Mechanism to determine and produce the right inputs (the "causes"), you'll have the experience of "flow," self-acceptance and the satisfaction of effortlessly creating the results you want.

A powerful and graphic demonstration of this principle may be seen in balancing a baseball bat, as mentioned in Chapter 2.

You'll be able to balance the bat as long as you keep your eyes and attention on the top of the bat (the "effect")—i.e. the bat's center of gravity being in a state of balance. When you move your eyes and attention to the way your hand is supporting the bat (the "cause"), you'll notice that you're immediately unable to keep your hand reacting fast enough to keep the bat in balance. Move your attention back to the other end of the bat (the "effect"), and, even though you're not watching your hand or conscious of what it's doing, your hand moves automatically as needed to keep the bat in balance. It's much easier to balance the bat when you keep your attention on the "result" and leave the "doingness" to your Creative Mechanism.

6

It's "User-Friendly"

There's no instruction manual required. Just ask your Creative Mechanism what you need to know.

LEST YOU get the idea from all of the motor-skill examples I've used so far that the Creative Mechanism operates only in the motor-skill area, nothing is further from the truth. I learned how to consciously trust my Creative Mechanism in gymnastics about forty years ago. I'm pleased to be able to say that I've now experienced consciously trusting my Creative Mechanism in other parts of my life. Just as in learning to use a hammer or a screwdriver, it's easier once you've experienced or "tasted" the tool in action.

Play another game with me, and answer the following questions:

1. What's your present home telephone number?
2. What'd you have to eat at your last meal?
3. What's the address of the house you lived in when you were going to grammar school?
4. What was the name of your best friend in grammar school?
5. What is 2 times 2, plus 4, divided by 4?

How'd you get the answers to those questions? They were probably just there after you read the question, right? Those answers had to come from somewhere. I submit that the Creative Mechanism part of your mind operates like a computer that has instant access to all of your past experience and training. Whenever a question is put to that Mechanism, it responds logically and literally to the best of the data and programming that it has in its memory. Test this concept by posing questions to it and noticing the first thoughts you get in answer to those questions. Didn't they copy the human mind in creating electronic computers?

When I did this question-and-answer process with my father a few years ago, he had difficulty recalling the name of his grammar-school friend. (At the time, my father was almost 81 years old.) I told him about this computer concept and to just consider that he'd put the question to his computer, trusting that he'd have the answer shortly. I then changed the subject of conversation to something else. Within five minutes he said, "Guess what, I just remembered the name of my best friend's father, but not my friend's first name." Then, right in the middle of telling me about the father, and what a famous man he was, the son's first name came to mind. My father was astounded at the process his mind went through, at an automatic level, to get that answer.

Can you remember how your Creative Mechanism has told you where you hid your keys, when you gave up trying to remember where you put them? How many times have you gotten an inspiration you needed during the middle of the night, while in the shower, or driving to or from work? I couldn't begin to count the number of times my Creative Mechanism has done that for me.

I remember many years ago seeing a movie about the life of Thomas Edison, inventor of the electric light bulb. Whenever Edison was stumped on a project, he'd lie down for a nap and awaken with the inspiration he needed.

The remarkable thing is that questions that need to get answered get posed in this same indirect way (i.e. without your conscious instruction) just because you've programmed yourself to succeed at the task you've undertaken. Having been pointed at the successful conclusion of the task, the Creative Mechanism, being the beautiful logic machine that it is, even takes care of framing the questions that are not seen at conscious level. It poses the questions that need to get answered in order to achieve the desired result.

For example, my father tells a story of how, when he was a young lawyer trying an important case, he awoke in the middle of the night before the day on which he had planned to "rest his case." He awoke with the realization that he'd not presented any evidence to establish an important element of his case. His Creative Mechanism had come to his rescue during his sleep.

There's this wonderful computer mechanism in that Creative Mechanism we each have that responds accurately to questions we give it, whether directly or indirectly. The trick is to train yourself to use it more deliberately and directly by more frequently noticing where you're pointing it, and to more consciously point it at what you WANT.

When I ask my Creative Mechanism a direct question, the answer will usually be contained in the first thought I have after I ask the question. Sometimes, however, the answer I get is that I don't know the answer. I can usually get around that by asking the question, "If I knew what the answer was, what would it be?" The computer in my head is honest, as well as logical. It will cough up the answer—or, if not the direct answer, it will give me the next question to ask, or where to look, that will produce the answer I need.

If what I notice is resistance to seeing the answer, I just ask, "What is the source of that resistance?" Then I take the first thought I get in answer to that question, even if it seems illogical. If I don't see the connection, I ask myself what the connection is and take the first thought I get. I keep asking, "What is the source of that?" to each answer I get, until I feel the release I need.

If I'm feeling down or depressed, I ask myself first, "What is it I'm feeling right now?" Then I ask, "What is the source of that feeling?" I usually get in touch with either a negative thought I had about myself, a picture of another person I've been imitating, an incident in my past, or an erroneous decision or belief under which I've been operating. Whatever answer I get, I ask: "What is the source of that?" Again, I may get a person, incident or belief. I keep asking: "What is the source of that?" until I feel the release. When I get to the TRUTH, I feel noticeably lighter. The important thing to remember is that you don't have to "fix" or dispose of the source—just acknowledge it and let it be.

I've found that literally writing down these questions and answers is an excellent way to engage my Creative Mechanism. I literally write: "*Q*: What am I feeling right now? *A*: Fear of failure. *Q*: What is the source of that fear?" etc., writing down the first thought I get in response to the question.

This technique really works for me. There is a very important ingredient, however:

YOU MUST ALWAYS ALLOW WHATEVER THOUGHTS YOU HAVE TO BE JUST "THOUGHTS." REMEMBER, YOU ARE ONLY MASTER OF WHAT YOU CAN LET BE.

If you resist the thought or make yourself bad and terrible for having it, you are giving it energy, form and life, and will find yourself at the effect of it and acting it out in some way. Remember, it's all only a piece of your history to which you've attached some undue significance. The "undue significance" is what is using up some of your Creative Mechanism's capacity. As soon as you can acknowledge the incident and allow it to be in the book of life that has your name on it, and without undue significance added to it, the charge on it will be gone. Your Creative Mechanism will then be freed from the necessity to keep some attention on or avoid that kind of item. You'll actually feel cleared and lighter. When you see and ACKNOWLEDGE THE TRUTH, you'll hear or feel the "ZAP!"

One of the most important things I got out of doing a lot of consciousness trainings was a heightened ability to observe my own mind in action in this way. My day-to-day experience during the past 15 years has been a laboratory in which I've repeatedly expanded my level of participation in life. At each new level I've experienced the anxiety that goes with the fear of failure, and each time I've discovered that if I had the courage to trust myself and keep going, things always turned out okay. The turning point in each instance seemed to be the moment when I remembered to ask myself what I was feeling, and then what pictures or beliefs I had that were the source of those feelings. As soon as I saw and acknowledged that "source," without needing to "fix" it, the unpleasant feelings disappeared and solutions showed up.

This observation of my own mind in action has led me to the conclusion that the control mechanism or "handle" to this magical tool in my mind is asking my "self" questions and paying attention to and acknowledging the answers I get. I've developed a great respect for this thing we call "mind" and now use it more consciously and deliberately to create what I want. You can, too. Like everything else you've ever learned, it just takes some "PRACTICE." (More on "practice" in Ch. 30.) Practice this technique by meditating for 20 minutes on the question, or by giving yourself instructions to sleep on it and awaken with the answer. You'll be amazed at the results you get from this.

I use this question-and-answer technique a lot in my work as a lawyer and writer. Whenever I'm "stuck" in writing a contract, I just back away from trying to figure out how to express what I'm trying to say, and ask myself: "What is it I really want to cover here?" Invariably, when I write down that question, and then its answer, the answer fits perfectly into the hole in my contract.

I also use this technique to get myself going on otherwise new and apparently impossible tasks. I remember the existence of my Creative Mechanism and then define the task at hand, along with acknowledging the facts and tools with which I must deal. Before I can say "Jack Robinson," I notice myself dealing appropriately with the matter at hand. I make my living as a lawyer solving multi-million-dollar real-estate problems with this simple technique. Whether you realize it or not, you're using it, too, in everything you do.

An example of this question-and-answer technique is how I started this book. I wrote the questions and answers down on paper as I went, starting with asking what I wanted to accomplish. I've reproduced them for you in the Appendix. If you read that question-and-answer sequence, you'll see that the answers I got are pretty close to the outline of this book. As I wrote and rewrote this book, new and additional insights, new ways of expressing old insights, and more clarity of purpose came to me (from my Creative Mechanism, of course).

There is a term now in vogue in the computer world for programs and systems that have all the help you need built into the program so that you don't have to keep resorting to the operator's manual. That term is "USER-FRIENDLY." The Creative Mechanism I've been describing is so "user-friendly" that whenever I don't know what question to ask myself, I refocus on my purpose and then ask my Creative Mechanism: "What question should I ask in order to accomplish that purpose?" It invariably gives me the question, the asking of which gives me the answer I need. For my money, the Creative Mechanism is the most effective and USER-FRIENDLY mechanism on the planet. It's a good thing that it is, because, as Bucky Fuller pointed out, there's no operator's manual provided with each Creative Mechanism.

7

Road-Map Logic

The CHOICE of what you want identifies your destination. The acknowledgment of where you've been up to now identifies your starting point. The determination of the necessary path between those two places happens at the automatic reflex level.

THE COMPOSITE definition of *CHOICE* is simply: "To select or make up one's mind from alternatives."

Applying that to creating what we WANT means we CHOOSE by making up our minds as to which result we WANT to have out of the infinite possibilities we can imagine.

A graphic, but simple, illustration of the importance of identifying what it is you WANT is the use of an ordinary road map. If I gave you a map of California, identified point *A* as Los Angeles, and asked you to determine whether you should travel north, south, east or west to get from point *A* to point *B*, you'd ask me to identify point *B*.

Forgetting the previous example, if I asked you to determine the direction in which to travel from point *A* in order to reach point *B*, and I identified only point *B* as San Francisco, California, you'd ask me to identify point *A*.

The message here, of course, is that, in order to have any success getting where we want to go, we always have to know BOTH where it is we want to end up (point *B*) and where we're starting from (point *A*). This is even more evident when we're using computer mechanisms to chart our course. Your Creative Mechanism operates just like the computerized guidance systems that get our space vehicles to predetermined orbits and back. The best of these systems must be given accurate information (i.e. the "co-ordinates") as to the location of BOTH ends of the trip to be effective.

CHOOSING where you want to go, or what you want to accomplish, will define point *B* for your Creative Mechanism.

If you have any difficulty defining point *A* (where you've been up to now), it may be helpful to ask yourself questions like:

1. What circumstances do you have in your life right now that would be replaced by *B*, if you had *B* now?
2. What pictures do you have or are expecting to happen that are the source of these present circumstances?
3. In other words, how have you really seen yourself with respect to having what you want up to now? (Remember, it's not necessary to "fix" or "handle" the old "stuff," just to identify and acknowledge it.)
4. Is that what you WANT? (If not, RECHOOSE what you WANT and see yourself relating to and experiencing THAT, NOW!)

Although we don't seem to give the *A* stuff as much attention as we give the things we say we want, identifying and acknowledging *A*-type items is as important as identifying the *B*-type items.

I suspect that there are at least two reasons why we shy away from looking at *A*-type items. First, we think we have to "fix," "handle" or "eliminate" the old stuff, and that looks too difficult or painful. And second, we intuitively use our not being able to identify *A* as a way of keeping us "safe" from the risk of failing to create *B*.

I hope you can see that if you're relying upon a computerized guidance system to effectively get you from where you are to any other place or level, you MUST give that guidance system accurate information as to the identity and location of BOTH ends of the trip. The necessary trajectory is then easily determined at the automatic reflex level.

Trajectory is defined in the dictionary as: "The path of a moving particle or body, especially such a path in three dimensions."

Isn't it interesting that the dictionary defines that word in terms of three-dimensional paths? *Trajectory* is the perfect word to describe the path we human beings take through the universe during our lifetime. And that's a computerized process.

(See Figure 4 for a graphic illustration of the importance of identifying both ends of the trip in order to create the trajectory required to complete it.)

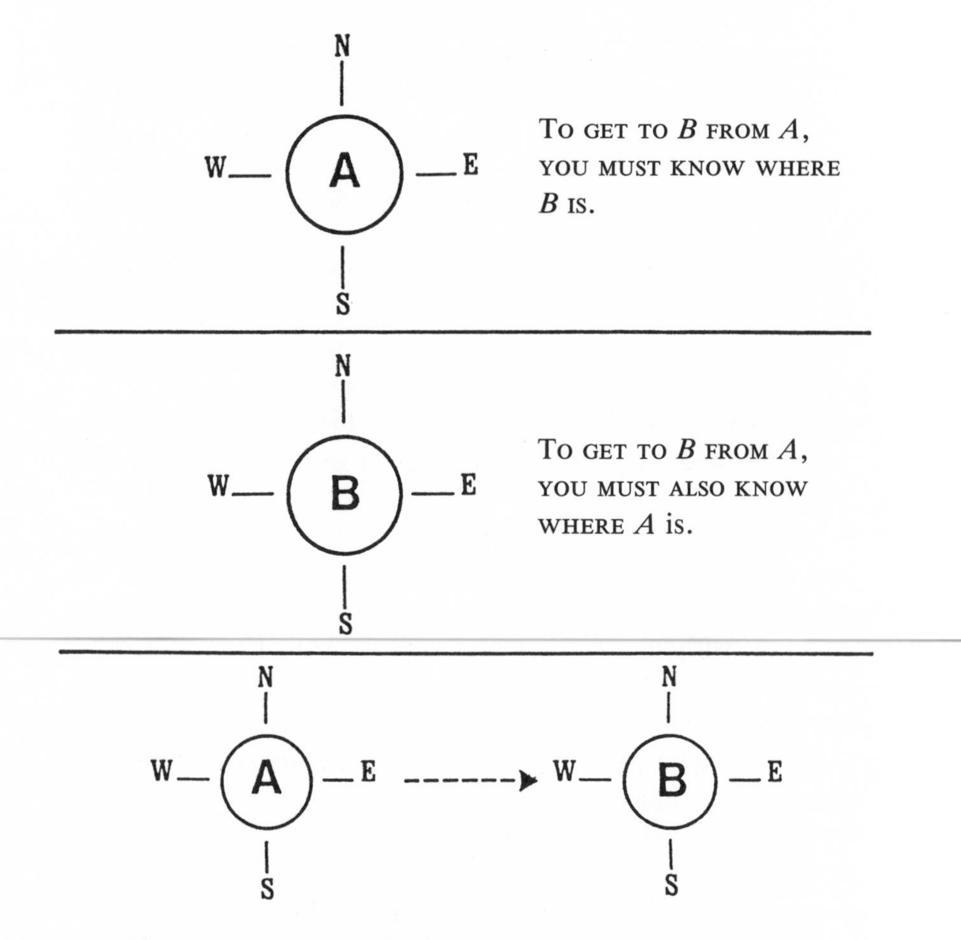

Figure 4. It Takes Both Ends of the Trip to Identify the Path between Them

8

“Rev” Your Engine

“Someday” is always “tomorrow.” Mock-up, contemplate and rehearse pictures of yourself experiencing the desired result as already accomplished—i.e. NOW.

When I was learning things like gymnastics and skiing, I noticed that I did not achieve any degree of proficiency in those activities until I had enough exposure to them to know what the “real McCoy” looked like. It was only then that I was able to see myself in my own mind’s eye actually doing those things. Mentally rehearsing a successful result, as if I were watching a movie of myself doing it, was present in every instance.

Remember how you learned to ride a bicycle or snow-ski, for example. You saw other people doing it and then imitated what you saw.

Many years ago Maxwell Maltz wrote in his now famous *Psycho Cybernetics* about basketball players who were able to improve their accuracy in free-throw shooting by just mental practice, without even touching a basketball. I’ve experienced similar improvement in my banjo playing just from mentally playing along with a cassette tape while driving to and from work. And we’ve all heard of athletes in many countries today using this kind of technique—visualization of successful and exceptional performances—with remarkable results.

I have presented these principles to a number of high-school typing classes and watched their typing speeds increase by as much as twenty words per minute from one lecture. What most produced that kind of result was the kids' letting their fingers go (trusting their Creative Mechanisms to take care of the "HOW") and mentally rehearsing the improved result they wanted. (Throwing a few candies into a paper bag with their eyes closed seemed to help a lot, too.)

I'm convinced, and science has established, that mental practice gives the Creative Mechanism the same kind of refinement of experiential data that would be obtained from actual experience. As we saw in a child's learning to walk, it requires a certain amount of "data" in the Creative Mechanism of what doesn't and does work, in order for the Creative Mechanism to refine and adjust its responses to the degree necessary to create "walking."

Richard Bandler and John Grinder, in *Frogs into Princes* and other works, recommend that, in order to create a new behavior pattern, you literally mock it up in each of four aspects: visual, kinesthetic, auditory and olfactory. They call this *Neuro Linguistic Programming* or *NLP*. The more vivid a picture you give to your Creative Mechanism, the more likely it is to produce that picture for you. Ask yourself the question, "What would it look, feel, sound and smell like if I had what I wanted?" Then mock that up in your mind's eye as a present reality.

In other words, just mentally contemplate and REHEARSE IT!

Fill out the "Rev Worksheet" at the end of this chapter with respect to something you want. It'll assist you in crystallizing a picture of it and facilitate your creating it.

I saw a piece about the brain on public television a while back in which films of brain scans were shown depicting areas of the brain actually "lighting up" just before the corresponding motor activity took place in the body. The commentator said that it has been scientifically established that the brain actually and literally "rehearses" the chosen physical activity in this way before the actual activity takes place in the body. Therefore, it is the "mental" CHOICES we make that our brain rehearses and which precede and initiate the whole creative process. If you don't believe me, the next time you go to the bathroom notice how you first see yourself doing in your mind what your body then manifests.

A composite definition of the verb *rehearse* is "to bring to a state of flawless, accurate complete being through repeated and habitual experience (real or imagined); to exercise repetitively and habitually."

Use the acronym *REV* to remind yourself to repetitively REV your Creative Mechanism, so to speak, as you would REV your automobile engine before moving to a new location. The letters in REV, spelled backwards, stand for *Visualize, Experience,* and *Rehearse*. REV will help you remember to mentally REHEARSE as vividly and as often as possible the fruition and present existence of what you want to create.

That's how you communicate to your Creative Mechanism the coordinates of where you WANT TO GO.

However, human creativity literally only produces what you point it at. Point it at something defined only in terms of the "future," and the ultimate result is always going to be only "someday." *Someday*, like the carrot on a stick, is always just out of reach. (See Figure 5.)

And as we mentioned in Chapter 4, what literally tells the Creative Mechanism to "start" creating is the addition to the rehearsed picture of the element of its being here NOW. That is the most subtle and overlooked aspect of the human Creative Mechanism. This powerful cybernetic guidance system is pulled into present action *only* when the result chosen and rehearsed includes the element of *NOW*. As Robert Fritz so beautifully teaches in the DMA program, if we hold and reaffirm the vision as a present reality, no matter what the circumstances, the obvious disparity between that vision and our reality pulls us into the behavior that will make the reality conform to the vision.

Snap your fingers "someday." Snap your fingers "NOW."

Figure 5. "Someday"

Notice the difference in mental process that goes with those two results. The more you practice acknowledging the existence of your Creative Mechanism, the easier it will be, in the face of that left-brain perception of the old inconsistent reality, to have the courage to contemplate and rehearse what you WANT as here NOW. It will never be now, however, unless you include "NOW" in the instructions you give your guidance system.

IF NOT NOW, WHEN?

REV WORKSHEET

What I Want Is:	
What Having or Being It Now Looks, Sounds, Feels and Smells Like: (In present tense—e.g. "I am" or "I have")	
The Next Step to Take or Thing to Do to Create It Is:	

DATED: ______________ SIGNED: ________________________

9

Love Yourself

Loving yourself just the way you are now sets you free from the need to operate from "victim." It gives your Creative Mechanism the important coordinates of where you're starting from and the worthiness to have what you WANT.

I USED to think that our need to operate from "victim" in manipulating others was the basic source of everybody's negatively oriented behavior patterns. Then an insightful friend of mine had the courage to point out to me that there was something even more basic than that—*the need for love.*

I looked at my experience, and sure enough, the decision to operate from "victim" came from the experience that I got more attention from my parents when I "cried" than when I didn't. There's a funny thing about "victim." Being loved without "bad" stuff going on is illogical to a belief system that has been programmed to believe that you only get love and attention when you have something "bad" happen to you. That's an endless downward spiral. "Victim" begets "bad stuff," which in turn begets more "victim."

If you can rehearse in your mind's eye that you are lovable, and actually mock-up the experience of loving yourself, just the way you are, your Creative Mechanism won't need to resort to the creation of "bad" stuff to get some attention.

If you have difficulty loving yourself the way you are, imagine that you're outside of yourself, looking back at the person you really know yourself to be—that kind, considerate, loving, caring, compassionate, playful child you would manifest if it were safe to express that, and if you knew how to do it. Wouldn't you want to "play" with the person you really know is inside you waiting to be discovered?

At this time in my life I'm practicing choosing to love myself—that person I really am deep inside. I'm learning to trust my ability to create the "good" things I want, and to be bigger than any adversity that may come up along the way.

And, even more importantly, I'm discovering that I'm *not* my circumstances. Circumstances are merely opportunities to manifest myself in the universe through participation and interaction with them. What I am is a whole, complete, unique and miraculous human being that has all the experience of my fifty-nine years (and maybe some other lives as well) upon which to draw in that participation.

I'm not my mind. My mind is this unique cybernetic guidance system that I have. What I need to do is to be more conscious of what that is and where I'm pointing it.

Who I really am is that consciousness on the plane above my mind that dialogues with and instructs it. There's really nothing wrong with my mind. It's only doing what I've trained it to do. If I want it to do something else, I've simply got to point it in that direction more consistently.

I am who and what I am, and I perform according to the sum total of what that is. I trust my Creative Mechanism to deal with the circumstances, operating from the unique experience I've had, and in furtherance of what I've chosen as the result I want to achieve.

Hallelujah—I'm free at last!

If you believe in absolute free will and that your choices are not directed by subconscious influences, it is still necessary to let go of your judgment about the bad choices you've made, in order to get on with and choose what you want in the present. It is the acknowledging and letting go of the significance of the past that empowers your cybernetic machinery to create now. The past is "history." It cannot and need not be changed.

It is my belief, however, that even the choices we make are a product and function, at subconscious levels, of who we are and what we've already experienced. And this is so, even though it may seem at the moment of choice that we are exercising absolute free will. I find it helpful in forgiving myself for my past bad choices to hold them in a context of their being the natural expression of who I am and where I've been up to that moment of choice.

Either way, the important thing is to let go of the "past" and focus on the "NOW." I find it easier to surrender the significance of my choices when I remember that I am an expression of a much higher reality.

Remembering that you don't have to "fix" anything, forgive yourself for your past choices and failures. Acknowledge and love who you really are. As soon as you do that, your Creative Mechanism will have the coordinates it needs to effectively chart the course from there to who and where you WANT to be, and, even more importantly, the "freedom" to do that. That freedom only comes when you've let go of the past and see yourself as "okay" enough and "worthy" enough to have what you WANT now. So CHOOSE and REHEARSE yourself as OKAY and WORTHY right now, just the way you are, and then let go of the issue. There's nothing in you that needs "fixing." What you need is more conscious "pointing."

10

A Unique Four-Letter Word: "Want"

"Want" has four letters, but it's not dirty. Identifying what you WANT is what focuses your Creative Mechanism.

I'M USING the word *WANT* in this book in the sense of the dictionary definition: "*a.* To request the presence of; *b.* To seek with intent to capture."

A lot of people think of the word WANT as something "bad." They operate from the belief that to WANT something they don't have is a "no-no," or that to obtain what you want will be at the expense of somebody else.

I can just hear their well-meaning parents, in an effort to mollify their child's hunger for more of life, explaining that to WANT what they don't have will only lead to frustration and disappointment—so "don't rock the boat." To WANT something is to be avoided at all cost. It only leads to frustration.

However, the real truth is that the exact opposite is true. As we've already seen, it is literally this very CHOOSING and mentally rehearsing of what you WANT and do not now have that points your Creative Mechanism at what you WANT and creates it!

If we don't fall prey to the *I-don't-see-how-to-do-it* or the *What-if-it-doesn't-work* "prompts" that our minds throw at us, and just keep refocusing on and CHOOSING what we WANT (with trust in our Creative Mechanisms), we'll eventually create what we WANT and have CHOSEN. It's literally the defining of what you WANT that directs your Creative Mechanism to produce it.

I've heard a lot of people ask, "But what if you don't know what you want?" In my opinion, the reason people purport not to know what they want is that they're afraid they'll look foolish in daring to aspire to something they can't yet see how to produce. The recognition of the existence of the Creative Mechanism is what gives people the courage and ability to CHOOSE what they WANT and frees them up to participate more in life.

To bypass the "I don't know what I want" impasse, when that comes up, simply ask yourself: "If I knew what it was I wanted, what would that be?" And watch your Creative Mechanism answer the question.

Remember, your mind is a logic machine. Train yourself to notice even the minutest thoughts that flash in answer to the questions you ask it. Computer mechanisms are absolutely logical in their responses.

If you don't understand the answer you get, ask yourself the question: "What is the relevance of that answer?" or "What is the source of the resistance I'm experiencing to finding out what I want?" Don't try to "fix" or get rid of the resistance. Just acknowledge it, and let it be.

Then ask again, "What is it I really WANT?" If you keep getting resistance, just keep letting the resistance be, tracing the source of it, until you feel the undue significance of it clear. It is not necessary to consciously get rid of the resistance. Acknowledge it, and reaffirm the CHOICE of having what you WANT.

11

Clarity of Purpose

Without clarity of purpose, you might just as well be a ship under full power with no "rudder." Articulating "purpose" programs the desired result.

FROM THE discussion of the importance of being conscious, from moment to moment, of one's intended results and the simple road-map logic involved, it should be obvious how important clarity of purpose is to getting very far with any particular endeavor. My trusty dictionary defines *purpose* as "1. A result or effect that is intended or desired; intention. 2. Determination; resolution."

I have acted as a facilitator of a networking group and found that the group's statement of purpose, when announced at the outset of the meeting, invariably set the tone and determined the results of its meetings. I have practiced the technique of actually looking at and polishing up my statement of purpose when I write, or when I participate in any group activity. The results seem to flow more naturally when I load that information (i.e. a clear, positive statement of purpose) into the Creative Mechanisms of myself and my audience at the very beginning of my endeavor.

As already mentioned, very often, in the course of writing a complicated real-estate contract, I run into factual or technical problems that are conceptually difficult to treat in writing. When I reach such an impasse now, I just take another pad and write the question: "What am I trying to accomplish here?" Then I write the answer to that question as it comes to me intuitively. Invariably, that answer fits perfectly into and fills the hole in my contract. My claim to whatever fame I have as a lawyer is entirely due to my expertise in being able to perceive all of the many variables that go into a complicated real-estate contract, and to get them down on paper in a way that makes sense, flows, and is fair and reasonable to all concerned. I owe all that to my deliberate and practiced use of my Creative Mechanism.

Take the time to articulate your purpose, either individually or as an organization, clearly, completely, and not in negative, but in positive terms. "Massage" that until it feels clean and concise and has all the essential ingredients that are important to the result you want. Put it in writing and rewrite it frequently, even if you're not changing it. Acknowledge and announce it at the outset of all meetings or undertakings involved in that project. Just restating it at the beginning of each meeting or communication will work miracles for you.

Notice whether what you've articulated is the real bottom-line result you want, or whether it's a list of preliminary things that will have to get handled along the way. Remember, getting too stuck in how to create the details or "inputs" can get you chasing your tail. I've noticed that people very often unwittingly get sucked into aiming at something much less than the ultimate result they want.

The Creative Mechanism is very lazy and very literal. It will produce no more than what you point it at. Point your Creative Mechanism only at creating the "means with which" to produce the result, and all you'll get is the "means with which." If you want to have the ultimate result, aim not just at creating the "means with which" or "inputs" required to produce that result. WHY NOT AIM AT THE ULTIMATE RESULT? The "means with which" will get handled automatically AT REFLEX LEVEL in the natural process of playing the game identified as the result you WANT.

It is also important that you include all essential ingredients you want. As mentioned, the Creative Mechanism is very lazy. If you want a blue car, you'd better include the color "blue" in the picture you're holding of that car.

An important corollary of this principle is that you must watch more carefully the title or name you put on your organization or project. The title is seen repetitively by, and is a powerful message to, your and everybody else's Creative Mechanisms. Many well-meaning charitable organizations unwittingly title their projects in terms of the things they want to eliminate in the world. That keeps people holding pictures of what they're trying to change, instead of what they want to create. It takes a much greater effort to get the job done that way, and participation in those projects can be very "painful" because of the suffering constantly brought to mind by the negatively oriented titles.* Take care to have your titles make a positive statement about what you want to create.

If you notice your metaphoric "hose" pointing at what you want to eliminate, just ask your Creative Mechanism to tell you what the OPPOSITE of that is, and then make a conscious CHOICE to have THAT!

*Consider the difference in feeling you get from the title "The Hunger Project" compared with "Love Is Feeding Everyone."

12

"Pink Elephants"

What you have to "fix," "handle," "change," "break through" or "eliminate" become "pink elephants" you can't touch. When the "old stuff" comes up, just reaffirm your new CHOICE by refocusing on what you WANT.

If you focus on what you're trying to eliminate from your life, instead of on what you intend to create, you put pictures of what you DON'T want (instead of WHAT YOU WANT) in front of your Creative Mechanism.

Barbara Marx Hubbard said it beautifully and succinctly:

What gets your attention, gets you!

Don't think of a "PINK ELEPHANT"! What did you get a picture of? A pink elephant, right? If I now suggested to you that you should avoid or get rid of all the pink elephants in your life, your Creative Mechanism will be programmed to look for pink elephants to get rid of. Have you given pink elephants more or less significance in your life?

I read an article in the *Los Angeles Herald-Examiner* (October 14, 1984) by Gay Norton Edelman about the art of communicating with children. Gay wrote of two teachers leading their classes across a schoolyard that contained puddles of water. One teacher told her class, "Don't get wet." The other teacher told her class to jump over the puddles. Three children in the first class got their feet all wet. None of the children in the second class got wet.

The otherwise very logical notion that you must first eliminate, "fix" or "break through" what you perceive as obstacles or barriers to having what you WANT is a "trap." Your mind is so literally logical, that whatever you tell it to "not" do, it has to first do, so that it can then NOT do it. However, we never let it get to the "not" part.

Giving significance to the negative or unwanted aspects of anything literally gives the Creative Mechanism pictures of that thing as more important than what you want to have in its place. The more you "dance" around an obstacle or barrier by treating it as likely to have some noteworthy effect on your life, the more you tell the universe how important it is to you. By giving higher priority to the obstacle or barrier, you give it power over you. Even if you were successful in eliminating the obstacle or barrier, there would still be another step necessary to create what you WANT. Why deliberately go through two steps, when one step directed simply at what you WANT would be more effective?

As we saw in Chapter 5 (" 'Cause and Effect' in Reverse"), the Creative Mechanism is most effective in creating results when we allow it to create the necessary equal and opposite inputs at reflex level by focusing on the desired end result. If your focus is on how "bad" things are, however, or on how "difficult" it's going to be to achieve what you want, you're unwittingly making the whole process painful and more difficult.

The nature of your Creative Mechanism is such that when you focus it on the way things would look if the desired result were already accomplished, the Creative Mechanism automatically, and in natural sequence, choreographs for you all the things to do that will produce that result, including the dealing with or ignoring, as the appropriate case may be, any real or imagined obstacle or barrier that may be in your way. If you focus and relax, trusting the Creative Mechanism, it'll tell you which thing to do first, how to do it, or whom to call to get it done.

In jogging on a very windy day a few years ago, I had to pull my visor well down on my forehead to keep it from being blown off by the wind. As a result, I could see only about five or six feet of the ground in front of me at a time. I noticed that out of not being able to see the horizon (which included the distance I had yet to travel and the steepness of the inclines I was approaching) I was less tired by the run. The whole thing just seemed easier.

From this experience I learned that the Creative Mechanism works best at automatic, reflex level with calm, relaxed and unexaggerated significance given to the difficulty or obstacles perceived to be involved in achieving the particular result. And remember how, in Chapter 3, we learned that we could be more effective if we literally "closed our eyes" to how difficult the task at hand looked, trusting our Creative Mechanism to take care of the "how."

Another reason why trying to fix, get rid of, or break through an old belief system, pattern, or habit—in order to have the space for a more appropriate belief, pattern or habit—doesn't work is that by using that approach you're trying to change history. Whatever the old belief, pattern, or barrier appears to be, it only exists in the present by virtue of your memory of the experience of it. It is therefore, by definition, something from the past, and just "history," unless you choose to repeat it in the present. You literally cannot touch the past. Trying to touch and "fix" or eliminate history is like trying to touch a ghost.

The fact that you (or anyone else) may have done a certain thing a certain way many times before (and you think that is your or their pattern) does not preclude you or them from CHOOSING a different behavior the next time. Remember, no matter how many times in a row you get "heads" in flipping a coin, the odds are still only 50/50 you'll get "tails" on the next flip. There are still only two possibilities—heads or tails. Where your life's experience is concerned, IN EACH MOMENT you literally have your CHOICE of whatever are the infinite number of possible responses and results you can imagine.

The "bad news" is that if you've been a "fixer" or a "breakthrough" artist up to now, you've been unwittingly making "pink elephants" out of your obstacles and barriers by giving them undue significance.

The "good news," however, is that the positive possibilities for the present are unlimited, depending upon how much you're willing to stretch your imagination. It's just a matter of CHOOSING which possibility you WANT to happen.

You don't have to do anything to your old pattern before choosing to install a new one, any more than you have to get rid of the darkness before you choose to turn on the light. Reprogramming your Creative Mechanism works like recording on magnetic tape. Whatever you record over the old material automatically replaces whatever data or programming was there before. The way you record or program a new pattern or intended result (albeit on top of an old one) is simply to let go of your thoughts about what you DON'T want, and CHOOSE, CONTEMPLATE and REHEARSE what you *DO* WANT.

Your old "pattern" will then invariably come to mind and sort of tap you on the shoulder to say, "You've always used me for this kind of circumstance. Don't you want to use me now?" All you need to do with that is thank your mind for giving you the opportunity to verify your NEW CHOICE before recording over the old response. Any decent computer program comes with that kind of built-in protection against losing old programming. The fact that your mind brings up the old response doesn't mean you're stuck with or "addicted" to it. It's really just another demonstration of the logical way your mind serves you by giving you "prompts" about how you handled similar circumstances in the past. It's just giving you the opportunity to verify your CHOICE of response this time, just the way a computer program prompts you with "Y/N" before letting you record over anything. It's just performing its "logic" function.

As a matter of fact, not only do you not have to do anything with the "old stuff"—if you DO engage or worry about the "old any way, you're just giving your Creative Mechanism of what you DON'T want, and making them more significant and harder to disengage.

Furthermore, depending upon how big the old pattern is, it may take only two or three instances in which you "practice" the kind of conscious choice to pursue a NEW PATTERN in order to establish it. That's really the essence of what "practice" is.

For example, some time ago I noticed on my way home from visiting my parents that the only time I visited them was when I had something to complain about and needed their sympathy and reassurance. Having noticed that, I remember making the conscious choice to let it be okay that I did that in the past and to be only positive about myself in their presence from that time forward. However, the next time I was with my father, I noticed myself still running my "poor me" on him. Interestingly, this time I noticed myself doing that WHILE I was doing it, and still could not stop doing it. Again, I just acknowledged with a bit of a chuckle to myself that there I was doing "poor me" again, and reaffirmed my CHOICE to only be positive about myself in his presence.

The next time I was with my parents, I noticed on the way home that I hadn't run any "poor me" on them at all that time and generally don't do that anymore—or if I do, I notice it and am able to stop it in the act. If a good Jewish boy like me can that easily record over the "poor me" pattern, anything is possible.

Another important aspect of staying focused on what you WANT is that, unless you have really CHOSEN a new bottom-line vision, the initial success will not endure. The new bottom-line vision must be inconsistent with the picture that produced the things of which you're now trying to rid yourself, or the changes won't last. The old vision will just create new circumstances that are as bad or worse for you to deal with as the old ones were.

For example, people who diet and exercise to deal with their weight problems very often gain the lost weight right back, unless they're able to CHOOSE and hold onto a vision of themselves as a thin, attractive, okay person worthy of having the good things in life. I've heard of many instances, on the other hand, where people who had discovered their own "okayness" just lost weight without even trying.

Similarly, attacking and eliminating the existence of all nuclear weapons only treats the symptom. It doesn't cure the disease. Until such time as a critical mass of the people on this planet envision us all living together in harmony and friendship, we will find some other device (probably more devastating than nuclear weapons) with which to threaten and kill each other.

(It is my sense that such a critical mass has already been achieved. People from all countries are reaching out to each other more and more each day, and the Presidents of the United States and the Soviet Union are now expressing optimism about the prospects for a lasting peace. I experience the evolution as already well in progress. What we need now is to spend more energy and technology on things we have in common as human beings, and on community needs, like mass transit, public and ecological health, and inspiring individual participation. The weapons issue will atrophy in due time, if we can reaffirm humanitarian values and principles.)

13

Choice

"Commit" and "decide" can be button-pushers. "CHOICE" is what best points the Creative Mechanism.

WHEN I realized that I couldn't *consciously* create the "doingness" of how I did anything (because the doingness always takes place only at the automatic reflex level), I realized that I'd wasted an awful lot of time and energy trying to figure out "HOW" to do things before choosing them.

Thinking that I had to see the "HOW" first, before committing to a particular result, meant that I'd probably spent my entire adult life being afraid to look at what I REALLY WANTED. Since I couldn't see the "HOW TO DO IT" immediately at hand or within my means, I was just going around in circles, looking for a place to hide—a place where I didn't have to risk failure.

I suspect the whole world is stuck in that rut.

How can anyone "commit to" a vision they can't see how to produce? For me, to "commit to" a particular result meant that I was *absolutely* responsible for creating it. I wasn't about to "commit to" something I couldn't see how to create.

The fear of failure or of looking foolish that is so prevalent in our culture keeps us from making responsible commitments. Without the awareness of the nature of the Creative Mechanism, our inherent guidance systems will reject as illogical the suggestion to "commit to" creating something we can't see the "how to do it" of in advance. Asking people to make that kind of commitment will either scare most of them away or add undesirable pressure and stress to what could otherwise be a simple, flowing kind of experience.

The word *commit* seems to tell the Creative Mechanism that there is something it's supposed to consciously figure out how to do and then do.

The word *decide* has similar problems. It comes from the Latin *decidere* which means "to cut off, determine." *Deciding*, therefore, seems to have implicit in it the selection of something at the expense of, or in opposition to, something else. It literally means to replace something with something else, literally "cutting off" and ending the former something—as in *insecticide*, *homicide*, and *genocide*. There is an element of resisting the former something in this perspective, which, as we saw in Chapter 12 ("Pink Elephants"), tends to actually keep that former something stuck in place.

CHOICE, on the other hand, simply means "to select from alternatives." There are no hidden negative instructions to the Creative Mechanism in the word *CHOICE*. A more consistent use of it is the secret to success.

So CHOOSING, CONTEMPLATING and REHEARSING the desired result, coming from trusting your automatic guidance system to discover what it needs, is readily accepted by the Creative Mechanism. You need only to keep refocusing on your vision and CHOOSING, CONTEMPLATING and REHEARSING it to eventually bring your reality into alignment with it.

The thoughts you CHOOSE and hold have a very magical quality. First, they will result in your own behavior being more consistent with what those thoughts are projecting as to who you are and what you are worthy of. As we'll see in Chapter 17, that makes a powerful statement to the universe, which it then mirrors. Second, your thoughts have a "magnetic" quality. They attract the circumstances that match the thoughts.

As Alan Cohen points out in *The Dragon Doesn't Live Here*

Anymore, the Latin roots of the word *circumstance—stantia* and *circum*—literally mean a thing that "stands" "around" something else. Alan saw an experiment involving iron filings on a metal sheet responding to various musical tones by arranging themselves in distinct patterns that matched the vibrational quality of the particular tone.

What if our thoughts project a similar vibrational quality into the universe (as I suspect they do)? Then, the way to get things to *stand around* you is to CHOOSE and hold thoughts of things the way you want them to be. If you do that, at the very least you'll notice your own Creative Mechanism moving you to the behavior (some of it very subtle) that will produce those results. And, if you're open to the possibility, the vibrations you produce may even work some magic, too. "Couldn't hoit."

14

Expectations

Is your basic expectation "effort," "struggle" and "worry"—or "fun" and "play"?

A WHILE back, I noticed that, even though intellectually I knew better, a lot of the time I was still habitually expecting the worst to happen. (That phone ringing is going to bring me some new problem I don't know how to solve, and more possibility of failure, etc.)

I also noticed a great reluctance to arbitrarily declare to myself that "good" things were going to happen. It seemed as though I'd not accumulated enough evidence yet for me to trust myself and the universe to produce the "good stuff." I still had to worry about, and get ready for, the adversity that was coming.

I asked myself what the source of that mindset was, and I was reminded of my old belief that life had to be an "effort" and a "struggle," which, in turn, stemmed from my early decision that to get taken care of in life, I had to cry first. Since I'd look foolish crying for no reason, I had to appear to be hurt or victimized in some way.

Most humans literally spend the first years of their lives getting their needs met by crying. Also, most of the role models they had to imitate were painfully efforting and struggling at the effects of their circumstances.

It's the damnedest thing. I've lived over fifty-nine years, and I can't remember ever having the "worst" that I worried about actually happen. Somehow, things have always turned out, to one degree or another. What more evidence do I need that it's safe to surrender and let go of the "effort," "struggle" and "worry" (the "victim" or "poor me") context from which I've lived most of my life? Acknowledging the existence of the Creative Mechanism, and how automatically it works, seems to make it more possible to make that surrender.

It is also important to take notice, from time to time, where you're operating on the "victim/fun" scale. A good way to do that is to simply ask yourself how much fun you're having in whatever it is you're doing or thinking at that moment.

The dictionary defines *fun* as "a source of enjoyment or pleasure." Can you hold all of the circumstances in your life right now as a source of enjoyment or pleasure without having to first change them in some way?

You may be noticing right now how difficult and irrational that seems. Yet it really is possible to hold life as the miracle that it is, and as an opportunity to be here and play with the circumstances it presents. I find myself being more able to do that, the more I write and talk about the nature of the Creative Mechanism.

I cut an article out of the *Los Angeles Times* several years ago about a man named Bob Basso who gives motivational speeches. The article quoted Bob (who at one time was an aide to John F. Kennedy) as citing an incident in which, just before going into a high-level meeting on the Cuban missile crisis, JFK asked Bob to give him a joke with which he could open the meeting. When Bob asked JFK about the appropriateness of a joke at such a serious meeting, JFK's reply was, "You have to understand something: If you're not having fun, you're not doing it right."

If JFK can have "fun" with the prospect of Soviet missiles based in Cuba, surely you and I can have "fun" with the circumstances in our lives.

The degree to which you have difficulty holding your circumstances this way may be a tip-off to how programmed you've been to look for the "worst" in everything. For example, habitually looking for your mistakes about which to feel "guilty" keeps you pointed at where you don't want to be, instead of where you want to be. Are you someone who has been trained to look for things over which you must feel guilty? If you are, it's no big deal. Just notice and acknowledge that. Then, CHOOSE and refocus on what you WANT. Rehearse that right over the old guilt pattern.

The antidote is to literally say to yourself "I CHOOSE to have my life be *fun* and an opportunity to *play* with whatever is going on." By the way, don't be discouraged by the difficulty you experience in holding to that notion. As Mel Brooks' 2000-year-old-man once so eloquently said, "You don't forget a national anthem in a minute!" Remember, your mind's bringing up an old pattern is just its way of prompting you with what you did last time. You need only REAFFIRM your CHOICE of what you WANT NOW.

Just get in the habit of asking yourself the question more frequently, "Am I having *fun* right now?" WITHOUT having to "fix" it if you're not, just acknowledge where you are on that issue. Take a deep breath and choose to relax for just that moment. Postpone making any judgment about the significance of it all or what to do to "fix" it. Trust your automatic Creative Mechanism to appropriately handle the "things" involved, when your speculative and worrisome expectations are superseded by the real and essential truth about them.

The mind does not have to worry about, nor intellectually or consciously understand, how the things in the universe interact. The Creative Mechanism understands and will respond appropriately at reflex level to whatever the truth is, in the Cosmic sense, even if you're not conscious of what that is. To speculate in advance about what could go wrong risks interfering with the natural process involved.

As Robert Fritz so beautifully points out in his book *The Path of Least Resistance*, the movement among things in the universe will always follow the path of least resistance. So why not contemplate the path you want to follow as being the one with the least resistance? Visualize what you WANT as being EASILY created by your Creative Mechanism.

15

"Mastery" Becomes "Serenity"

"Mastery" is simply the art of being "as one with" things—letting go of their "good/bad" significance. That's really the experience of "love" and "serenity."

THE LITERAL composite definition of *mastery* is: the state of being in full control of, or having complete skill with respect to, something.

You can't logically be in control of, or have complete skill with respect to, anything that you regard as not okay the way it is. As we've seen, you are at the effect of anything that you need to "fix," "handle," or eliminate from your life. That you are master only of what you can let be, is really just the flip side of the principle that focusing on what you think you have to fix makes "pink elephants" out of them.

Each "thing" in the universe has its unique characteristics. When a particular thing is allowed to interact with any other thing, the critical characteristics of the two things determine how the two things end up relative to each other.

You and I are also "things" in this universe, in this simple, physical sense.

However, a unique and critical characteristic of us human "things" is that we have Creative Mechanisms. We also have a whole lot of physical and mental mobility and flexibility, including the ability to select and use all kinds of tools that expand and multiply our potential impact on other things. So, in this natural sense, we are a very special kind of "thing," capable of an exquisite and infinite variety of responses to the things with which we come in contact.

My study of the principles in this book has led me to a much greater appreciation of the kind of cosmic perspective of the "goodness" or "badness" of things reflected in the teachings and writings of people like Ram Dass and Alan Watts. They speak of planes of reality where "good" or "bad" really isn't an issue—where things just are what they are, in their highest natural sense. I particularly love Alan Watts' description of how we would never try to tell a cloud that the way it has shaped itself was not okay, and that our human behavior is no less a natural phenomenon than clouds doing what they do. I find it very interesting that my analytical search for greater effectiveness in my everyday circumstantial reality has led me to a heightened appreciation of, and surrender to, the miracle of my just "being." But that's exactly what's happened. The answer I got to the question "How can I be more effective in life with less effort and struggle?" is "Surrender the significance of the daily circumstances to the higher power, and come out and play more HERE and NOW." And that does not stop me from supporting and pursuing those things I consider to be "good" on this everyday plane. On the contrary, it frees me up to participate in those things all the more.

No matter how "bad" a thing is, *if* you can just let it be whatever it is, without exaggerating the "significance" of it, you'll notice your Creative Mechanism producing the behavior, at the automatic reflex level, that is most appropriate for your interaction with that particular thing and your ultimate objective.

I grant you, that there are things that can happen to us that we would all agree are very "bad"—even life-threatening. Yet, the Creative Mechanism seems to jam up when we habitually react to the adversities and obstacles of everyday circumstances as life-threatening. And, even in life-threatening situations, we are more effective if we can stay calm. If you can let your Creative Mechanism do what it does best, being the cybernetic device that it is, *it will always produce the behavior most consistent with your past experience, your present expectation of the result you want, and the characteristics of the other "things" at hand with which you must deal.* The only element of that formula over which you have any conscious control is the choice you make as to what you want and expect to happen. If you react to any situation with the exaggerated significance of its being life-threatening, you jam up the machinery.

Real "mastery" is, therefore, the art of letting yourself and everything else in the universe just be and do what they do, without exaggerating the "good/bad" significance of any aspect of the process. If we make the "badness" of anything significant, we are making a statement to the universe that we feel threatened by that thing—that we do not trust ourselves to deal appropriately with it at reflex level. That seems to have implicit in it the need to get rid of or "fix" that thing. As we've seen, that perspective just tends to keep the thing stuck in place.

This phenomenon explains why, as many people have observed, history often repeats itself. Once a thing is judged as significantly "bad," we tend to keep looking for more evidence to prove and support our judgment about it. This tends to create new instances that perpetuate the old judgment. The traditional judgments about each other among the various ethnic groups of the Middle East are typical examples of this phenomenon. For this reason, it is important to give less significance to where you've been, and more to where you WANT to be NOW.

All things will naturally deteriorate and die or fade into the backdrop, according to their essential nature, if negative energy is not added to them by our own need to prove them "bad," or to "fix" them. Think of the last time you hung a new picture on the wall. You were conscious or aware of its presence for about two hours. Then, before you even realized it, unless there was something about it that you didn't like, the picture was just part of the wall or backdrop.

Whenever I think about the principle of letting things dissipate of their own nature, I get a picture of a balloon that I've blown up and left untied, and the way it behaves when I let go of it. It quickly dissipates itself according to its own form and energy. Most things in the universe will not disappear quite that quickly. But they'll either disappear on their own, or our Creative Mechanisms will assist them to disappear, if we can just let them interact naturally with each other at reflex level.

Another traditionally troublesome attitude about "mastery" is that it is usually considered as requiring actively and consciously "doing" something to achieve the desired state of "control" over things—in other words, manipulating things. However, as we've just seen, in terms of conscious attitude it's just the opposite.

Also, many of the things we habitually label as "bad" or "wrong" are really only somebody's judgment of whether they like that thing or not. For example, to me the best part of my daily shower is when I turn the faucet abruptly to the full "cold" position. Most people I tell that to shudder. Yet, to me a cold shower is invigorating to the point where, in the summer time when the cold water isn't very cold, I miss the "coldness." For most people, "cold" is "bad." And the same is true of "pain." The literal and naked truth, however, is that both "cold" and "pain" are the signals of the presence of valuable negative feedback. My nervous system reacts to a cold shower with an increased metabolism and feelings of invigoration. And I've even trained myself to view the cold water as having healing qualities.

Similarly, the pain experienced when you put your hand on a hot stove helps you know that your hand should be moved before you get burned. Pain in your body is a signal to notice that you are doing or thinking something that is inconsistent with your peaceful and harmonious survival. That's valuable information if you're paying attention.

If our most effective interaction with things takes place at the Creative Mechanism level anyway, exaggerating our judgment about a thing as "bad," or "wrong," in the sense of whether or not it conforms to our society's agreements, or whether it threatens the success of our expectations or our life, doesn't add anything to our ability to deal with it. On the contrary, the resistance that is implicit in the exaggerated significance we attach to "bad" things tends to lock them in place.

Use your impulse for "bad" or "make wrong" judgments as signals of the OPPORTUNITY to practice "mastery"—i.e. *trusting your Creative Mechanism to deal appropriately with the circumstances at hand.* The only technique I've found that works in those instances when I feel threatened by something is to literally "be as one with" it. I mean, I literally send those "bad" circumstances that frighten me "LOVE." I've found that to be an effective way to achieve "mastery" with respect to things by which I feel threatened. I'm now working on staying in that state of mind more of the time and not feeling the need as much as I do. That's my next lesson.

In looking at this perception of "mastery," I asked my Creative Mechanism to tell me what state of mind would better facilitate my being able to more consistently practice what is really intended by the term *mastery*. The answer I got was *SERENITY.* A composite definition of *SERENITY* is: the state of being calm, appropriate, emitting and reflecting light, happy, cheerful and intelligent.

From now on, I'm working on CHOOSING, REHEARSING and PRACTICING being in a state of LOVE and SERENITY at all times and with respect to all circumstances. I choose to have LOVE and SERENITY be my basic ground of being.

16

Sweet, Sweet "Surrender"

"Pressing" for results comes from lack of trust. "Surrendering" the significance of the outcome is what empowers your Creative Mechanism.

As a reminder to be aggressive, etc., I used to have a little sign that said "GO FOR IT" hanging on the inside doorknob of my front door. I now use the back of that sign on which I've written the word "SURRENDER."

Whenever I talk about the importance of "surrender," I'm reminded of an incident that happened to me when I was about 13 years old. On this occasion I was in the surf at Ocean Park Beach when the waves suddenly got so turbulent that I could neither get up on the shore nor under the waves to calm, deep water. I struggled vigorously to get free from what I perceived was the threat to my survival—*the turbulence*—first in one direction, then in the other. With no success, I literally gave up, thinking I was about to drown.

The wave I surrendered to tumbled me around a lot, but it also carried me far enough ashore that I was able to crawl out of the water on my hands and knees. I've always had a sense that there was a valuable lesson in that experience. Too bad it took me 40 years to understand what it was.

If we exaggerate the significance of our "good/bad" judgments about an aspect of a situation (I got frightened by, and reacted to, the turbulence), we react to the "what if" and get noplace. Surrender to the intuitive (I instinctively rolled myself into a ball), and you get better results (I was carried ashore by the underlying current of the ocean).

I learned a beautiful way to demonstrate this principle from a man named Ralph Strauch, who gives Feldenkreis workshops. The particular demonstration I have in mind involves putting a volunteer in a chair and having him or her first demonstrate that he or she knows how to stand up from sitting in that chair. Ralph then stands behind the seated subject and places the bottoms of his forearms heavily upon the subject's shoulders.

He then instructs the subject to stand up while he, Ralph, is presenting this downward pressure on the subject's shoulders. Invariably, the subject perceives the downward pressure as an "obstacle" to getting up, and the first reaction is to try to get away from the downward pressure by slouching in the chair. This movement naturally requires the lifting of the feet as a counterbalance to the slouched upper body. Now, obviously there's no way anyone can stand up while their feet aren't touching the floor.

Remember, the instructions were simply to stand up, and what the subject has just done is lift his or her feet off the floor. The subject invariably gets sucked into dealing more with the perceived obstacle than with creating the intended result of standing up.

Ralph then repeats the experiment, but this time telling the subject to focus his or her attention on a spot across the room and seeing himself or herself at that spot. Even though there's the same downward pressure on the shoulders, the subject plants his or her feet on the floor, leans his or her center of gravity forward, and stands up. Ralph's downward pressure on the shoulders has absolutely no effect on the subject's ability to stand up when the subject stays focused on the desired end result—being across the room.

As discussed in the previous chapter, each thing in the universe has its own unique characteristics, and each of us human beings is a "thing." In this same physical sense, we are subject to the same laws of nature. When we surrender to the nature of things to be what they are and do what they do, our Creative Mechanisms are most effective. They are then free to operate without a lot of "What if it doesn't work?" kind of negative expectations being fed into them. If you allow your computer-like Creative Mechanism to do its job, it will take into account the essential nature of all "things" with which it must interact on the way to the chosen result, and will automatically calculate and produce the unique behavior required of you.

The automatic nature of your Creative Mechanism gives you as much flexibility in responding to obstacles you encounter in your daily life as the "fluidity" of water gives water the ability to flow over and around, and even carry with it, the obstacles in its path to the sea. I can see now why Lao-Tzu's "Tao Te Ching" philosophy I've long admired draws so beautifully on the nature of water as a model for human behavior. (As interpreted by Archie J. Bahm, "The best way to conduct oneself may be observed in the behavior of water.")

While jogging recently, I was thinking of how seeing myself as "fluid" as water had helped me around a particularly difficult situation at work, and the following line came to me: "My thanks to Lao Tzu, the philosopher who first said we should emulate water." What a great beginning for a poem, I thought. But how'm I going to create something to rhyme with "water" and still keep that meter? I just kind of turned it over to my Creative Mechanism, and within two days I had the following poem:

OUR "FLUIDITY" IS OUR DIVINITY

My thanks to Lao Tzu, the philosopher who
First said we should emulate water.

I can be more serene, now that I've seen
O'er and around is the way that I oughta

Just be with the blocks, that seem hard as rocks,
Trusting my natural "fluidity."

There's nothin' to "fix" when I can just get my kicks
From expressing that inherent Divinity.

Several years ago, while I was working as an executive in a packing-house and making myself wrong for having run away from law practice, I heard about the importance of "surrender." For a year after that, I struggled, to no avail, to understand how surrendering to *where I was* could get me to *someplace else*. That was totally illogical to my conscious, rational mind.

Then I literally gave up trying to figure that out and accepted the probability that I'd be working in that packing-house the rest of my life. Within three months after I'd consciously surrendered to where I was, I was offered a job to practice real estate law in Century City (exactly what I'd previously envisioned and let go of).

Fourteen years later, I'm a successful senior associate with one of the largest and most respected law firms in Los Angeles. I work closely with and am highly regarded by the lawyer I most respect in the real-estate field in California. I got there by envisioning that result and then letting go of pressing to get there, by always moving forward to take care of whatever was in front of me to the best of my ability, and at the same time being willing to fail and dig ditches, if necessary.

I have a reputation for getting tough, complicated real estate transactions documented and completed on time, and I don't have any conscious sense of how I did that, other than by repeatedly choosing to let go of the significance of the outcome, and by trusting my natural abilities and instincts to get things done. (The interesting thing is that 30 years ago I was a painful procrastinator.) I still have my bell wrung a lot by the way I've been programmed to initially exaggerate the significance of things as life-threatening, but I've learned to pay more attention to my instincts in dealing with things, and to give up the significance of the result.

I hope you can see that the "surrender" I'm talking about here doesn't involve giving up participating in life, as most people construe it. On the contrary, it means giving up the burden of self-doubt and worry about the significance of the result. It means PARTICIPATING, not less, but MORE!

Surrender means loving and trusting your self and your Creative Mechanism enough to risk participating in life with *more* freedom and "fluidity." It means having FAITH in and TRUSTING yourself and the universe.

Given that your Creative Mechanism is really a cybernetic guidance system, the more you just surrender to, and "hang out" with, a particular "thing," the more accurate and complete will be the data your guidance system obtains about that thing. The more data your guidance system has about any "thing," the more effective will be your cybernetic response to it.

You are therefore not disabled by surrender. On the contrary, your creative machinery is literally EMPOWERED by it.

Ram Dass tells the story of a Japanese boy who asked a Karate master how long it would take him to become the finest Karate expert in the land, if he studied with this master. "Ten years," was the reply. "That's a long time," said the boy. "What if I worked twice as hard as the other students?" "Twenty years," the master said. "What if I studied day and night?" said the boy. "Thirty years," was the answer. The boy then said, "How is it that each time I say I will work harder, you say it will take longer?" To which the master replied, "The answer is clear. When one eye is so fixed on the destination, there is only one eye left to find the way." What the master is saying by this metaphor is that if you become too obsessed or preoccupied with the result, your natural ability will not be fully present for the process of creating that result.

So, there must be a calm about the way we hold the vision of the desired result. The key is to mentally rehearse ourselves having what we want; but then it is critical that we relax, allowing our *full* creative capacity (our Creative Mechanism) to address and take care of the "how" at reflex level.

Many ancient orders advocate renouncing earthly pleasures and quieting the mind as the path to enlightenment—thereby achieving that state of surrender where there is little or no traditional significance to any "thing." Although the beauty of a mountaintop can inspire a broadened perspective, we don't literally have to put ourselves in a monastery to celebrate the miracle of which we are a part. In fact, I suspect that the need for such formal "renunciation" of worldly pleasures is just another more subtle way of giving power to the pleasures.

For example, in the Bhagavad Gita it is said, "Be not identified with being the actor, and be not attached to the fruits of the action." The wisdom in that advice is accurate but makes "pink elephants" out of what we're *not* supposed to do. Expressed in positive terms, it should read something like:

1. Experience yourself as "one" with and as an expression of everything in the universe. (A lot of people would call that "God.")

2. Celebrate and take advantage of the opportunity to participate. Experience with joy and pleasure the miracle that is your very existence.

What the Bhagavad Gita is really trying to say is PARTICIPATE in the world. As Jesus put it, "Be in the world, but not of the world." Be willing to just be alive and playin'. As we'll see in the next chapter, there's even more powerful magic in that than you might suspect.

Another piece of ancient wisdom oft quoted in this context is the admonition "There's nowhere to stand." Again, translating that into "positive" terms, it's really just saying, ***BE WILLING TO STAND ANYWHERE!*** **The WHERE really isn't significant.** ***PARTICIPATING*** **is what counts!**

You can step out of the significance of the circumstances game at any time by simply choosing to recognize your sense of family with, and fluidity with respect to, all "things" in this universe. I like to think of that as just "being as one with" (my definition for *being in love with*) something. It's sometimes hard to do, but I've found the practice of embracing obstacles, upsets and adversities in the "loving" way water would embrace them to be an effective way of getting to the kind of surrender that empowers my Creative Mechanism. Use your upsets as the signal of opportunity to practice this kind of surrender. Send the cause of your upsets *love*. Be as one, or "family," with them. Flow with and around them.

I know that may sound irrational, but then that's exactly what this book's all about—getting from the need for overrationalizing to trusting your intuitive and cybernetic self.

In cosmic terms, whatever judgments anyone could make about the significance of your circumstantial success or failure are totally meaningless and irrelevant. It should therefore also be irrelevant to your own sense of "okayness" and well-being. You are not your wealth or your circumstances. Given the nature of the universe, whatever happened or happens was and is the product of the interaction of the critical characteristics of all the things involved in that process. There's nothing for you to do except play your unique part in that process. Who you are and even the very CHOICES you make are also a product, as well as a part, of that same process. All you need do is ask your higher self to tell you what your purpose in this life is, and what positive focus will best manifest that. Then, just keep "playing"—taking care, at reflex level, of the business at hand to the best of your present ability.

Mahatma Gandhi also spoke about surrender in a beautiful way. He said:

> *God demands nothing less than complete self-surrender as the price for the only real freedom that is worth having. And when a person thus loses himself, he immediately finds himself in the service of all that lives. It becomes his delight and recreation. He is a new person never weary of spending himself in the service of God's creation.*

The only real freedom that is worth having requires the surrender of the self-oriented "good/bad" value system. When you find that state of mind, you find yourself as one with, and in the service of, all things in this universe. That has literally been my experience. Even with my agnostic upbringing, the more I look, the more I find myself acknowledging that greater, higher reality most people call "God." I now use reminding myself of that truth as a means of recapturing this sweet state of "surrender."

I define *surrender* as the giving up of the significance of the circumstantial outcome and the need for conscious control of my process, loving myself enough to trust this incredible universe to turn out appropriately for the good of all things involved—including myself.

Out of this inspiration I have written some poems I find very helpful in achieving this kind of "surrender" when used as a mantra. I recommend them to you as such:

I celebrate all circumstance
As part of God's Great Plan.
I love myself and trust myself,
Just the way and who I am.

I SURRENDER

My highest Truth I now call "God."
That I so long overlooked this, does seem quite odd.

For the beauty I now see, astounds me.
You see, the Miracle that is God, surrounds me,

And the Love that is God, embraces me,
Giving who and what I am, the space to be.

The Spirit that is God, flows through me.
And when I acknowledge all this, it renews me.

The Truth I now see in "God" inspires me.
I surrender to God, entirely.

Every human thought, act and heartbeat is no less an expression of that highest Truth most people call "God" than is each ripple on the ocean or cloud in the sky.

All of life should be experienced as a flight around the world in a small airplane. As observed by a friend of mine who recently got his pilot's license, the joy in flying is not so much in getting to your destination as it is in experiencing the miracle of "flight."

17

The Magic of Participation

Participating in the world—that is, projecting your essential characteristics into the universe—will determine where it puts you.

As I've mentioned, the critical characteristics of the things interacting with each other literally determine the results of the interaction. It should be noted and emphasized that it is the free "interaction" that makes that happen. Since you and I are also "things" in this physical sense, for each of us to find our natural place in the universe we must interact with the things around us. That means "participating" in the world.

In case you've any doubt about the accuracy of this phenomenon, I've found a way to demonstrate it. Somehow, in the course of a conversation about how important it was to project one's self as "BIG," my mind brought up a picture of how when I used to smoke cigarettes I always found small particles of tobacco at the bottom of the package. Somehow my mind calculated from that phenomenon that if the fine particles of tobacco work their way to the bottom of the package, the larger particles would always end up on top.

Experimenting with this notion, I put two distinctly different-sized steel ball bearings (quarter-inch and sixteenth of an inch in diameter) into a small pickle jar. I found that if I jiggled the jar so that all of the ball bearings interacted gently with each other, the smaller bearings ended up on the bottom, and the larger ones (notwithstanding their greater weight) on TOP.

What's literally happening in this jar is that the smaller bearings are falling through the spaces between the larger bearings and accumulating on the bottom of the jar. As the smaller bearings accumulate on the bottom, they naturally have the effect of pushing the larger (even though heavier) bearings to the top. (See Figure 6.)

As long as there is the appropriate amount of gentle, persistent interaction, the ball bearings will always order themselves in this way, according to their critical characteristics—in this case, their relative size. (The greater weight of the larger bearings only seems to be critical if there is violent motion of the jar whereby the bearings become airborne and lose contact with each other. Then the weight *does* become the critical characteristic.)

If you have any doubt about this principle, take some blended tea and dump it into a plastic sandwich bag. Bounce the bag a little and notice how the various sizes of tea leaves order themselves in layers.

So, too, will all things in the universe, including you and me, order themselves, *if* there is enough gentle and persistent interaction—i.e. participation. When you and I consistently let people know the truth about who we are, they will naturally treat us according to where that fits.

Interestingly, where human beings are concerned, there is an extra potential in that we have the power to IMAGINE and CHOOSE from an infinite number of possibilities how we want to present our beingness to the universe. The universe will respond, not according to what we say, but according to what it sees and feels us projecting in our behavior. As Jesus put it: "Wherefore by their fruits ye shall know them." So too, you and I will end up, in relation to the rest of humanity, according to the statement we make about ourselves by our behavior.

For example, the way we carry our bodies (what is commonly known as "body language") makes a strong statement about our competence. How and when we talk, and what we talk about, make important statements. In business negotiations, I frequently notice that the party who compulsively has to make a lot of unnecessary "table talk" generally comes out on the short end of

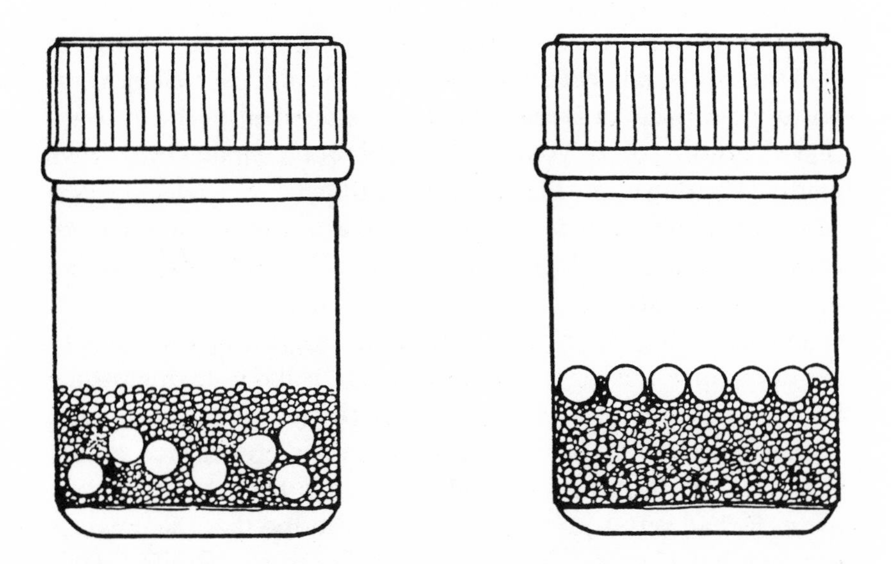

If you shake the jar vigorously up and down, the 10 larger balls go to the bottom. Jiggle the jar gently and persistently so that all balls gently interact with each other: The 10 larger balls will rise to the top. Thus, with gentle, persistent interaction the bigger things rise to the top.

PRINCIPLE: Participate in the world and it will put you where you fit according to what you project.

MORAL: Choose what you want to project.

Figure 6. It Takes Participation for You to Find Your True Place

the deal. Even performers who need to talk a lot about themselves between songs are unwittingly making a negative statement about themselves to their audience. The big stars I've seen rarely talk about themselves between songs. I can't remember seeing Michael Jackson talk at all between songs. Be aware that overselling yourself or your product is really making a statement to the universe that you think you or your product isn't good enough on its own merits. The universe will respond accordingly. Whereas, the person who is calm and to the point makes a subtle statement of competence and confidence in himself and his position to everyone in the room.

The key things here are, first, seeing what it is you want to project yourself as being—and that even includes distinguishing between whether you want to be an auto mechanic or a lawyer. The next thing is to project competence and confidence as that person. And, third, let the world know what that is by living your life as if that were a present reality. You'll find that the universe responds quickly and appropriately to the way you manifest yourself in deed.

A number of years ago I went to a seminar on prosperity where I was told to always carry around a hundred-dollar bill, and to cash it at least once a week. Here I was, already a fairly successful lawyer, but I noticed that I felt funny carrying around and cashing that big a bill at my neighborhood restaurant or grocery store. But I did it anyway. It didn't take long before I, and the universe, saw me as somebody *worthy* of carrying around that kind of money. My yearly income is now probably double what it was when I first started carrying that big bill. And now I feel funny unless I'm carrying several of them.

Another very effective way to let the world know who you are is to participate in the things you love to do and/or do best. That's where it will be the easiest to demonstrate competence and confidence, and achieve quicker success. Also, you're more effective if you don't go for the proverbial "moon" or "bomb" on every play, but rather settle for the five-yards-and-a-cloud-of-dust kind of success. In football, five yards on every play guarantees you a touchdown, whereas going for the "bomb" tells the other team that you don't have confidence in your ability to move the ball in a normal way. That not only gives the other team confidence, it tells your own teammates and Creative Mechanism that you don't believe in them or yourself. It also adds undue "significance" to the outcome.

Many coaches make this same subtle mistake by substituting players unnecessarily, or sending in "brilliant new" strategies, at critical moments, not realizing that they're subtly making a statement to the players in the game that they don't think the players can do it on their own. The person at the head of any organization always sets the tone or context for their "players" in this way. I'm told that John Wooden of UCLA basketball fame, during time-outs at critical moments of key games, talked about things the players were to do during the following week that were totally unrelated to the significance of the moment. What a powerful statement of confidence that made to his players' Creative Mechanisms!

Remember, also, that it's "monkey see, monkey do." It's not so much what you say you intend that determines where the universe puts you, but rather what it experiences you are actually projecting about who and what you are, and your worthiness and readiness to have what goes with that. So, when opportunities in which you said you wanted to participate come your way, choosing to take advantage of them makes a powerful statement.

Start right now by just noticing what you've been telling the universe about yourself by your behavior. For example, which face shown in Figure 7 are you presenting to the world? Notice the difference in feeling conveyed to the universe by something as simple as the shape of the mouth in these drawings.

The MAGIC in CHOOSING to PARTICIPATE is twofold. First, you're giving strong messages to your Creative Mechanism that you mean business about what you said you wanted, and second, the universe responds more to what it experiences is the

Figure 7. Which Face Are You Presenting?

"truth" about you. I recommend that you get in the habit of writing down every night before you go to sleep all the things you did or the CHOICES you made that day that were consistent with, and in furtherance of, the things you WANT. You will be astounded by what seem like miracles coming out of the blue to support your progress.

So, just the way the small ball bearings push the larger ones to the top, the universe will let you know what you've been telling it about yourself by where it has put you up to now. Look around and see where that is. If that's "bad news," don't despair.

The "good news" is that you have the inherent ability to IMAGINE, CHOOSE and REHEARSE yourself as being who or where you want to be. If who you are or where you find yourself is not who or where you want to be, just acknowledge what you've been projecting so far, and RECHOOSE, CONTEMPLATE and REHEARSE a present experience of being NOW who or where you WANT to be.

Remember, however, that always going for the "big one" can make a negative statement to the universe. Mastery and serenity come from surrendering the need to exaggerate the significance of any particular earthly circumstance. The real joy in life comes from participating in life's process by manifesting your unique self to the fullest, right now. It is not the magnitude of any particular circumstantial result. Doing what you love to do and do best, in this present moment, is what creates the most magic and personal satisfaction.

18

Celebrate Your "Response-Ability" Now

It's easier to take responsibility for your life when you realize you were born with "response-ability" as part of your inherent Creative Mechanism. The CHOICE to CELEBRATE your barriers and patterns NOW is what puts you into a state of "mastery."

STEPHEN R. COVEY in his book *The Seven Habits of Highly Effective People* accurately points out that the word *responsibility* is really just a contraction of "response-ability." That's exactly what your Creative Mechanism gives you: **THE ABILITY TO ALWAYS RESPOND APPROPRIATELY AT CYBERNETIC AND REFLEX LEVELS.**

Now that you know your Creative Mechanism takes care, at cybernetic and reflex levels, of the "doingness" of everything you do, participating in and celebrating your life should be a whole lot easier. That's the only real "doingness" there is for you to do in the whole process, anyway—to make the CHOICE to LOVE and trust yourself, and to BE HAPPY, *RIGHT NOW!* Remember, "someday" is always *tomorrow*. HAPPINESS is not the product of having or doing the right things. HAPPINESS is a state of mind you can only achieve, no matter what the circumstances, by CHOOSING TO BE HAPPY!

To that your mind probably says, "But what about all the old barriers and patterns I have to first handle?" A workshop leader I once had named Hal Isen said something about handling old barriers and patterns that has stuck with me like glue: "THROW A PARTY FOR THEM!"

This is a very simple but powerful metaphor. Throw a "Celebrate Your Barriers" party and make everybody who shows up write down one of their old barriers or patterns on some toilet paper as the ticket for admission. As we saw in Chapter 12, what you think you have to fix, handle, change, get rid of, resist, etc., becomes a "PINK ELEPHANT" you can't reach. The positive opposite to getting rid of something is to literally throw a party for it and "celebrate" it. What you can *celebrate* you'll not be *resisting*. You'll respond to it most appropriately at reflex level, and everything will turn out in the normal course of events. I recommend that you get in the habit of using the word *celebrate* a lot. The use of it has been pivotal in my growth.

Practice making the CHOICE to CELEBRATE THE MIRACLE THAT IS THIS MOMENT OF YOUR LIFE!

If you look up all the words in the definitions of *celebrate* and *barriers* and then combine them, the composite definition or explanation of the advice "celebrate your barriers" would look something like:

> **Take notice of the structures, boundaries, walls or limits you have constructed to bar your growth, with deferential regard, joy and gaiety.**

You can never be at the effect of anything you're celebrating. You'll always be in "mastery" with respect to it.

Here are some of the beliefs and patterns I noticed were barriers for me when I asked myself the question: "What is the source of my unwillingness so far to have what I want?" Perhaps you've had some of these beliefs:

1. I'm not supposed to have it that "easy."
2. My life has to be full of hard work, effort and struggle for me to be worthwhile and okay in the eyes of others.

3. I have to do it this way to please my father, because it wouldn't look good for me to have it easy when he efforted so.

4. I don't know what else to do.

5. I don't know how to do it any other way.

6. I don't know what to do to change it to the way I would like it to be.

7. I'm afraid to take risks or fail.

8. I'm afraid to make a mistake—I will die or be disgraced forever in my father's eyes if I make a mistake.

9. I wouldn't be able to get sympathy and attention any more—i.e. operate from "victim."

As you can see, a lot of my issues revolve around my relationship with my father. You can substitute "mother" or anybody else for "father."

Think of your barriers and patterns as "PINK ELEPHANTS" and throw a party for them. They'll be a whole lot more lovable and easier to celebrate that way.

Remember, all you need to do with them is acknowledge that they've been a part of where you've been up to now. That acknowledgment enables your "response-ability" to effectively chart a course from there to where you want to be. Loving and *celebrating* your barriers and patterns is what releases you from being at their effect and sets you on your way to what you WANT.

That calls for one helluva CELEBRATION!

19

"Zig Zag's" All There Is

There's no such thing as a perfect straight line—"zig zag's" where it's at.

ANOTHER MINDSET I've noticed that's very common in our culture is the belief that we must look for the perfect, or what I call the "straight-line," solution to the question "HOW DO WE GET THERE?" That is, if we're at point *A*, wanting to get to point *B*, we assume that there's a perfect, straight-line course between those two points for us to discover and follow. We're traditionally reluctant to venture off point *A* until we can see the straight line course to Point *B*.

The straightest of lines under a strong enough microscope will show a wiggle someplace. There's no such thing in the universe as a perfectly straight line. That being the case, consider the futility of instructing a computerized guidance system to find and pursue a perfect straight line that does not exist. The experience of looking for the perfect solution is the experience of effort and struggle, without much movement or actual participation.

You may've noticed how trying to "figure" things out very often has that kind of frustrating quality about it. You may also have noticed how, when you gave up (literally surrendered) trying to "figure it out," you got the inspiration you needed. How many times have you found your keys or remembered someone's name or phone number or gotten the idea or inspiration you needed that way?

The secret to a satisfying life is to find something you can get excited about and move in that direction with as much enthusiasm as you can muster.

The German poet Goethe said it correctly:

> *Whatever you can do, or dream you can, begin it. Boldness has genius, power, and magic in it.*

If you did that, you'd realize after a while that there were some aspects of the universe you hadn't seen or taken into account when you chose your original objective. You'd eventually have to adjust direction to allow for that new information. After another while, you'd probably adjust again, and then again, and again and again.

To some observers it would appear that you were very uncertain about what you wanted to accomplish. These observers would've missed entirely the overall distance you'd have traveled from point *A* in the general direction of point *B*, and the valuable experience (data) you would've accumulated along the way about what does and doesn't work in life. (See Figure 8.)

Also, consider the powerful statement you are making to the universe and to your own Creative Mechanism about who you are and where you intend to end up, à la the "Jiggle Jar" principles of Chapter 17.

It's also interesting to note, as we saw in discussing the dynamics of walking, that "progress" always involves first putting one's self *out of balance in the direction of the intended destination* and *then* bringing up the point of support. There's nothing wrong or bad about missing the mark a few times. In that process, your Creative Mechanism learns what it needs to know about that part of the universe in order to refine its responses enough to meet your specific objectives.

I'm told that guided missiles are actually ALWAYS off-course and self-correcting, right up to the moment of impact with their targets. If you think about it, I think you'll see that so are you and I—ALWAYS! Examine your experience of driving an automobile or riding a bicycle—or even walking. Do you realize how much you already "zig zag" through life? Notice how you trust

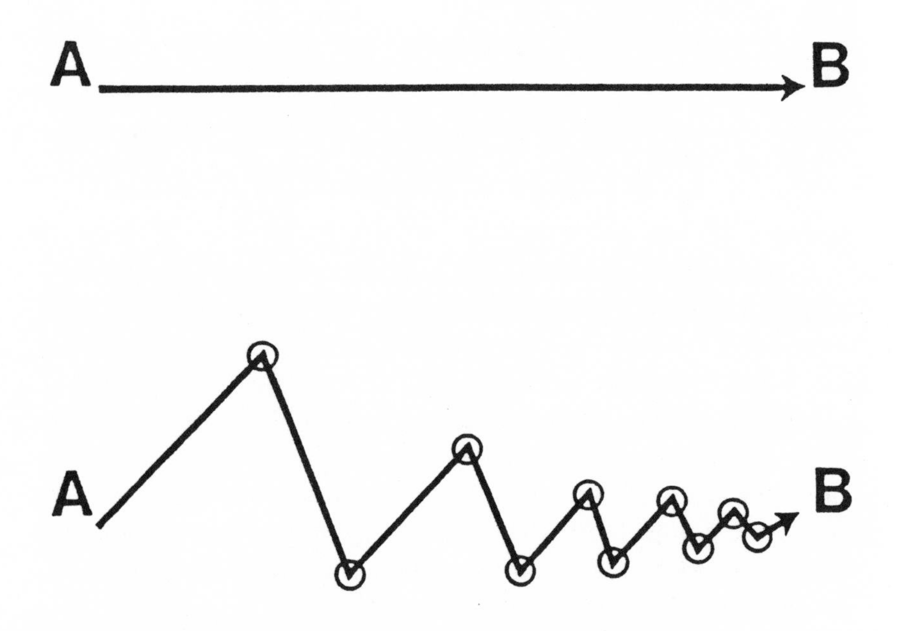

Figure 8. Zig Zag's Where It's At

(Each change in direction—the circles—represents a piece of new experience for your data bank.)

your Creative Mechanism when you drive your automobile at 70 miles per hour, allowing your automatic reflexes to move the steering wheel back and forth and operate the gas, brake (and maybe clutch), as required.

Somehow I suspect that if a guided missile could judge itself the way we do, it wouldn't be worrying very much about its "imperfect" trajectory, the way you and I do. I suspect it would just keep moving forward, trusting its inherent guidance system to do what it's programmed to do—i.e. use the "negative" feedback as valuable information from which to adjust course in the direction of the CHOSEN result.

Also, it must always be remembered that the measure or quality of one's life is not a function of how many, or what kind of, point *B*'s we achieve, but rather *how fully we participate* and manifest ourselves in the process.

I recently noticed another aspect of "zig zag" that rather startled me.

I saw that my life was a "zig zag" all right, but I wasn't zigging and zagging TOWARD something. I was zigging and zagging AWAY FROM the possibility of failure. I'm certain that a lot of you can relate to that one.

How many of us are interested in finding a place of equilibrium in which to "hover," instead of seeking new levels of participation? Ask yourself whether your life is about avoiding disaster, or about going TOWARD something you're excited about. There's no such thing as *hover.* We're either going *up,* or we're going *down.* It's your choice. Take your pick.

Henry David Thoreau, in *Walden* (1854) put it thus:

> *If one advances confidently in the direction of his dreams, and endeavors to live the life which he has imagined, he will meet with a success unexpected in common hours.*

And remember, as we said in Chapter 17, the magic is not in the results. It's in the *participation.* The joy and quality of life lie in merely "ziggin' " one more time than you've "zagged." So, keep on "ziggin'!"

Since I started practicing the awareness of, and putting trust in, my Creative Mechanism, the amplitude of my "zigs" and "zags" seems to be reducing, and I give less and less significance to the outcome. Life is so much more fun that way.

20

Be Your Unique Self

Allow yourself to do it your way, and acknowledge what that is.

AN IMPORTANT adjunct to the technique of participating and being true to your real self is allowing yourself to do whatever you do in your own inimitable fashion. Let go of the necessity to live up to your pictures of the way you think someone else would do it, or the way you would do it if you had your own act really together.

Given who you are, you really can only do whatever you do, anyway. No matter how hard you may struggle, you can only bring to bear at any given moment the sum total of your unique being and experience. To ask your Creative Mechanism to do otherwise is to give it unnecessary work to do.

Jamaal Wilkes, of UCLA and Los Angeles Lakers fame, was one of the most consistently accurate shooters in the game of basketball. In fact, Chick Hearn, the announcer, often referred to Wilkes' 15-foot jump-shots as "Wilkes' layups." Yet Wilkes had this unorthodox style of bringing the ball around and releasing it from behind his head—even while shooting free throws, when there is no reason for him to do it that way. Wilkes told me that he developed that style as a kid in order to avoid having his shots blocked by larger opponents.

When Wilkes played for John Wooden at UCLA, coach Wooden let Wilkes shoot the way he shot. Many coaches would've been tempted to try to impose their own notions of the right way to shoot baskets on Wilkes. Wooden wisely let Wilkes go with what worked for Wilkes.

If what you're doing works—that is, you are getting the results you want—keep doing it that way. Do MORE of it, until the universe tells you to do otherwise. It will respond and let you know when that is. If what you're doing isn't working, do something else.

For myself, I've noticed that I used to spend a lot of energy thinking that I was supposed to be everything to everybody, and particularly a more knowledgeable lawyer than I was. I had habitually overlooked who I really was and what I DID know, to focus on and worry about what I thought I didn't know. Look at where that pointed *my* creativity "hose"!

When I asked myself what the source of that belief was, the answer I got, again, was the belief that life's supposed to be a struggle. When I asked myself what the source of *that* belief was, I got that I'd chosen to operate from "victim" and "poor me," and that was how I saw the people around me operating.

I NOW RESOLVE TO ACKNOWLEDGE MY UNIQUENESS AND THE CONTRIBUTION I MAKE TO THE WORLD BY PUTTING THAT INTO INTERACTION WITH THE UNIVERSE IN MY OWN INIMITABLE FASHION.

21

Vacuums Induce Expansion

Under pressure to achieve, all things tend to contract. In a vacuum they tend to expand. Create vacuums around yourself by letting go of the significance of "win/lose" and creating the atmosphere of "play" and "game" around your endeavors. Contributing to others is a key to expansion of the self.

THE SIGNIFICANCE we give the results of our endeavors has an important effect on the outcome.

For example, for a lot of people, focusing on "winning" comes out looking more like "not losing." We've seen that focusing on what you do NOT want, instead of what you WANT, points your Creative Mechanism at what you DON'T want. Those of you who follow sports will recall many instances where the underdogs won games they were not supposed to win. When everyone expects you to lose, you don't have to worry about "not losing" and can relax and let your real natural reflexes take over. (Remember, the Creative Mechanism is automatic.) Examples of this were the successes of first-year NBA coaches of the Lakers and Celtics, Pat Riley and K.C. Jones, whose teams won the NBA championship in their respective first years as head coach. No one expected a first-year coach to win a championship, so the pressure was off.

On the other hand, the favorite is under all kinds of pressure not to lose. The consistent champions are the guys who don't think in terms of winning or losing. They think in terms of playing and enjoying the game to the fullest extent possible at all times—i.e. they're just keeping their eye on the ball, so to speak, instead of on the outcome of the game.

Seeing a picture of one's self as the champion is helpful, but letting go of the significance of the outcome during the game is essential.

One of my students recently reported that he won a basketball shooting contest against a much better shooter by letting go of worrying about how impossible that looked, and instead visualized pictures of himself holding the winner's trophy. What a great metaphor!

See yourself holding the winner's trophy.

Remember, if you think in terms of what you're "supposed to" accomplish, or how difficult it looks, you're creating "pink elephants." With regard to any endeavor, just ask your Creative Mechanism to tell you what the "winner's trophy" for the desired result looks like, and then see yourself holding it. It's exactly this kind of indirect picturing that frees the Creative Mechanism up and points it at what you want to create.

What I consider to be the greatest example of success in one's chosen field is the success achieved by John Wooden as the coach of the UCLA basketball team during the period 1964–1975. John's personal vision was that doing your best to become the best that you are capable of becoming is more important than whether you win or lose the game. After 15 years of staying true to that vision, his team won the NCAA National Championship. His teams then won it almost every year until he retired (an astounding 10 championships in 12 years.) One of the two years he missed involved a last-minute loss in the quarterfinals. The other nonchampionship year involved the fact that his freshman team, which consisted of Lou Alcindor (Kareem Abdul-Jabbar) and four or five other high-school All-Americans, was the best team in the country and beat the varsity easily in the first practice game of the season. The varsity was not able to see itself as National Champion after losing to its own freshman team in its first game of the season.

John Wooden's success, and the way he achieved it, has been

a major source of inspiration in my life. I've savored the following newspaper quote from the LA *Times* a few years after John retired, when LSU won the championship:

> *Said LSU basketball Coach Dale Brown, explaining the success of the Tigers: "This team is relaxed and the brightest I've had here." He added: "I got to know John Wooden well and listened to much of what he said. I once asked him, 'How come you never got a smell of the national title the first 15 years at UCLA and then you won it every year?' He told me, 'You've got to relax and get the team to relax. It took me that long to learn to relax.' "*

Can you imagine, as I mentioned in Chapter 17, a coach having so much poise as to not even talk about the game during a crucial time-out of a championship game? That's what I'm told Coach Wooden had learned to do as a way of keeping his team relaxed.

The emphasis in John Wooden's program was on his players' working toward doing the best of which they were capable in terms of complete basic basketball, and the winning and losing would take care of itself. They played the game of basketball with a zest and style that thrilled everyone in the stadium. It was the way they played the game that inspired a new era in college and professional basketball. The ballet-like teamwork, the "full-court" participation, and the passes that nobody before Walt Hazzard had dreamed possible literally inspired the basketball world to a new level of excellence.

The starting lineup of that first Championship team had nobody taller than 6'5", but they were so focused on playing the game the way it should be played that lack of height was not critical. (Walt Hazzard, Keith Erickson, Gail Goodrich, Jack Hirsch, Fred Slaughter, Kenny Washington and Doug McIntosh, I salute you!) It is my belief that their pride and joy in participating to the fullest and in the pursuit of excellence and teamwork, while staying relaxed and detached from the significance of winning or losing, was the secret of their success. They worked hard in practice to develop the experience in the fundamentals, and trusted themselves to express that at flat-out, reflex-level participation at both ends of the court during games. They were rarely intimidated by the other team's reputation. They were a joy to behold.

If only we could operate in our lives the way the Wooden teams "full-court pressed" and ran the "fast break" on the basketball court! You can, if you just *let go of the significance of winning and focus on the joy of participating!*

Whenever I think of the undue significance we tend to give to results, I see the following analogy:

Visualize an airtight box approximately two feet square, and visualize that a blown-up and sealed balloon is resting inside this box. Let the box represent the purpose, goal or target you've chosen for yourself, and let the balloon represent you inside the context or "frame" created by that particular purpose, goal or target. (Every time you create a purpose, goal or target, you are really putting yourself inside of, and measuring yourself by, that purpose, goal or target, as though it were a "frame" or "box" within which you must then operate.) To the degree that you hold the success or failure of the outcome as a life-or-death matter, you are pumping air pressure into that box. The increased air pressure will make the balloon contract.

On the other hand, to the degree that you are letting go of the significance of the outcome, you are pumping the air pressure out of the box and creating a vacuum. The vacuum will make the balloon expand. (See Figure 9.)

If you can let go of needing to fix or improve your own personal circumstances and focus on contributing to others, you will take the pressure off yourself (in other words, create a vacuum around yourself). Taking the pressure off one's self will produce expansion, naturally, according to the laws of physics. My income and my participation level in life, both professionally and communally, have more than tripled since I got in touch with this

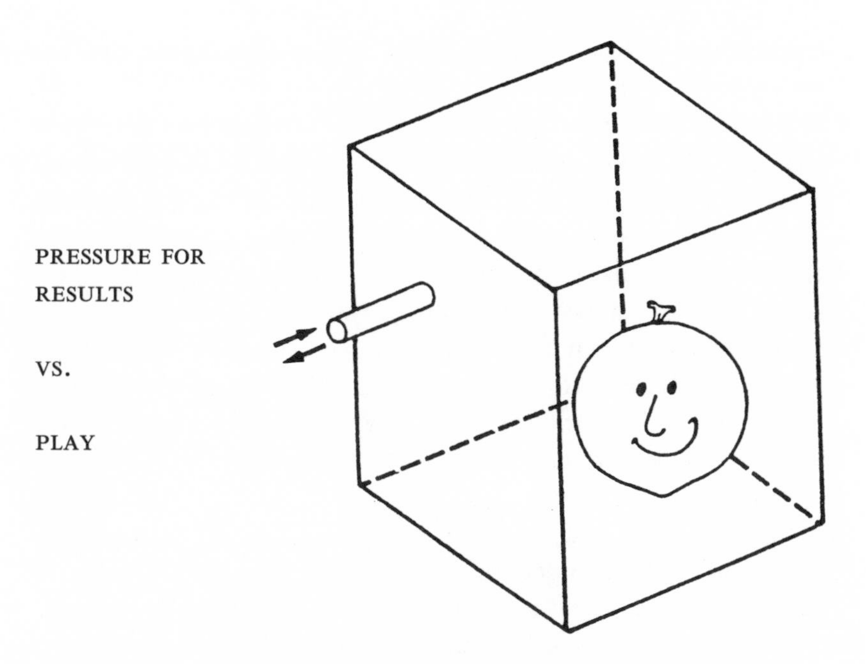

Figure 9. Create a Vacuum within the Framework of the Goal or Purpose You Are Pursuing by Taking the Significance out of the Result. Remember, Life Is a "Game." *Play* and Have *Fun*!

principle. And it all happened naturally, without my going hunting for it. As a matter of fact, whenever I tried to press for more or faster results, everything jammed up and stopped.

Now, whenever I notice that I'm efforting to figure things out or pressing for more, better or different results, I literally tell myself to surrender the matter to my Creative Mechanism, and just CHOOSE, CONTEMPLATE and REHEARSE pictures of the end result I want to happen—i.e. what me "holding the winner's trophy'' looks like—trusting my Creative Mechanism and the universe to do the rest.

When I first started experimenting with trusting my automatic Creative Mechanism I had difficulty trusting it. I asked myself what the source of that difficulty was and saw that I was giving a lot of significance to whether or not I achieved the result I'd chosen. When I asked myself what it'd look like if I didn't attach so much significance to the result, I saw that I'd already be in a state of ecstasy and not really NEED the result to be happy. That made it much easier to trust my Creative Mechanism to do its job. But then I had the thought that it was difficult to create being in ecstasy when what looked like ''bad'' things were happening to me.

I asked myself how you create ''ecstasy'' under those conditions and was reminded of the principle that contributing to others takes the focus away from one's self and tends to create a vacuum around the self. Contributing to others is probably the purest and most beautiful way to ''participate'' in the world. The best way I know of to create that self-expanding vacuum around yourself is to let go of needing to handle or fix your own ''case,'' and instead focus on contributing to others.

Reread the quote from Mahatma Gandhi at the end of Chapter 16, ''Sweet, Sweet 'Surrender,' '' and then watch the joy and satisfaction in your life expand.

22

Integrity with Life

If you clean up and complete the unfinished and incomplete things in your life, your Creative Mechanism will be more effective.

As WE'VE seen in Chapter 17 (''The Magic of Participation''), manifesting who you really are is what determines your place in the universe. And how you know what you've been manifesting is by looking at where you are—i.e. where the universe has put you.

To the extent you have any unfinished or incomplete business, details or space in your life, the ''real'' you is not being manifested. Anything your mind has categorized as ''unfinished'' or ''incomplete'' has been stored in your Creative Mechanism for future resolution. And probably you've also made a judgment about the item or yourself as being ''bad'' or not okay, by reason of that incompletion—e.g. a messy closet, a banged-up fender, an unpaid bill, a lie, a broken promise, etc.

Also, each and every item of incompletion in our lives is occupying a part of our Creative Mechanism's capacity that would otherwise be processing and producing the positive results we said we wanted. I envision our Creative Mechanism as having a finite capacity. In other words, it may have a 256K-byte capacity. Every piece of unfinished business stored for future treatment will use up some of that capacity. In addition, if we have some ''good/bad'' value judgment or feelings attached to the item, it will use up even more capacity. As you can see, the greater the number of unfinished, resisted or "bad" items you've stored for future treatment, the less capacity will be left available for creating the behavior needed to handle this moment, let alone what you want to positively create in your life.

Evidence of this phenomenon I think can be seen in what happens when you reduce the things you need to handle to a written checklist. I've noticed that most of the times I write a "to-do" item down, I remember it and get it handled almost automatically without ever again looking at the piece of paper on which I wrote it. I feel noticeably more relaxed, just having written it down. It seems that until I write the item down, a part of my mechanism is occupied in "remembering" something I have to do—or probably, more accurately, worrying about NOT forgetting it. The minute I've written it down, my mind seems to say, "Okay, you don't have to worry anymore about overlooking it." And again, "the load has been taken off my mind," so to speak. Literally, too, a part of my automatic mechanism has been freed up for more constructive duty.

Clean up and organize your life and your space, and watch your life expand.

23

There's No Such Thing as "Failure"

There's no such thing as "failure" if you're participating in life.

I'VE NOTICED recently that sometimes when I'm confronted with a new task that involves something I haven't done before, or that I think I don't know how to do or will have difficulty doing in the allotted time, there's a feeling of panic that sets in. When I ask myself what the source of that panic feeling is, the answer I always get is the fear of being a "failure" or of making a mistake.

A very successful motivational speaker by the name of Art Mortell defines *failure* (which includes making mistakes) as "an experience that turned out less than what you expected."

That's just another way of saying don't exaggerate the "good/bad" significance of things. After all, if we do what we do, and the universe responds the way it responds, at cosmic level, the result isn't "good" or "bad"—it just IS what it is.

By participating with any particular part of the universe we just learn more about the way it works. If we trust our Creative Mechanism to deal appropriately with those things we judge as "bad," there is really nothing to fear.

The fear of failing or making a mistake has been a biggy in my life. Our well-meaning parents and teachers, in their zeal to teach, unfortunately all too often come down hardest on what we did that didn't work (labelling IT and US as "wrong"), instead of reinforcing our participation and what we did that was RIGHT.

All my life I've avoided taking risks out of my fear of failing, and when I did take risks, very often the uncomfortableness produced by my facing the fear of making a mistake was excruciating. The biggest lesson I've had to learn in my life (and it's one that I'm still working on) is to really be able to participate more fully in life WITHOUT the compulsion to attach and exaggerate "good/bad" value judgments to the outcome or myself.

We learn about the universe only by interacting with it, à la Chapter 19 ("Zig Zag's All There Is"). And, like the guided missiles that we are, we really learn more from our mistakes (the "negative feedback") than we do from our successes. The trick is to let go of needing to constantly look for and avoid what we judge is "bad," and to participate more in life.

Participate means: "To take part; join or share with others."

If I hold being a *failure* as: "One who declines, weakens, or ceases to function," I can never be a *failure* as long as I continue to participate and interact with the rest of the world, especially if I'm acting with integrity with respect to my real self (i.e. what is in my heart).

Here's a poem about being with mistakes:

ON MISTAKES

I am who I am.
I do what I do.
So why should I question
What comes out of the blue?

Most of my life
I have seen only strife—
So fearful of error
  I've labored.

What a joy to behold
That the universe is gold,
When life without fear
   is what's savored.

"Miss" "takes" are not "bad."
They're just lessons I've had
'Bout things that are not
   all that sacred.

Things do what they do,
And the universe is new,
When as to judgment
All things are left naked.

I am who I am.
I do what I do.
So I won't question
What comes out of the blue . . .

—Unless I do!

24

Those "Awful Feelings"

Allow yourself to have "feelings." Acknowledge their source. Choose to have things turn out. Let go of needing things to turn out by focusing on contributing to others.

WHAT I'VE learned from studying my uncomfortable feelings and emotions is that they are really valuable gauges that monitor and reflect the degree to which I'm out of balance with the natural universe—i.e. the degree to which my conditioned response, and the "good/bad" judgment I've made about myself for having that response, are keeping me from serenity and being "in the flow" with the things around me. I grew up reading most of the challenges in my life as fraught with the possibility of failure. To fail or make a mistake was literally equivalent to death. It felt as if a vacuum hose was hooked to my rectum and sucking out my insides. Ram Dass refers to these moments as "Sturm und Drangs" (storms and stresses).

During the last few years I've noticed that wrestling with these compulsive feelings, and trying to get rid of them, always made them worse instead of better. I noticed that the only thing that ever freed me from the pit of despair and depression that went with those feelings was to surrender to having them—i.e. to let go of the "good/bad" judgment I'd made about myself over what had sourced them.

Your "sturm und drangs" are not who you are. They are simply the result of your mind prompting you to respond the same way you did last time. And the horrible feelings that go with those moments may be viewed in the same way you'd view the temperature gauge of your automobile, as it monitors and reflects the presence or absence of abnormal heat in your engine. They're just telling you it's time to CHOOSE a different response.

Over a period of years I've watched my mind deal with these Sturm und Drang kinds of feelings and jotted down the thoughts that helped me free myself from their debilitating effect. I find it very valuable to reread these thoughts when I notice myself struggling with, and beating myself up for having, those kinds of feelings again. Perhaps you will, too:

It's okay to experience feelings of uncomfortableness, anxiety, resistance, and depression. They are not anchors to the past, unless you fall into the trap of trying to "fix," "handle," "change," "eliminate" or "break through" them. In truth, they're just "PROMPTS"—signals of OPPORTUNITY to GROW and EXPAND your KNOWLEDGE and MASTERY by exercising your gift of CHOICE. Just throw a PARTY for and CELEBRATE those feelings.

REJOICE at the opportunity to experience yourself as big enough to INCLUDE those feelings by learning the lesson the universe is offering you in that process. Allow yourself to be "human"—that is, a being with a mind that gives you "prompts" and feelings that go with them. Those feelings are really just the symptoms of the exaggerated negative significance you associate with the thoughts or circumstances involved.

You are not your thoughts, circumstances or feelings. You are not even a "bad" person for having unpleasant or "bad" thoughts, circumstances or feelings. You're not a bad person for doing whatever you did that triggered those thoughts, circumstances or feelings. You did the best you could at the time.

Define and ACKNOWLEDGE the "bad" thoughts and feelings. Ask yourself these questions: (1) What is the picture I'm holding of what I expect to happen that's sourcing those thoughts and feelings? (2) What is the SOURCE of that picture? ACKNOWLEDGE and let that be. It's just a "thought." CELEBRATE and get in the FLOW with whatever's going on.

Your life will turn out according to the cosmic scheme of things, even if you have those thoughts, circumstances or feelings. BE IN THE FLOW with, and TRUST the nature of, all things in the universe. Trust them to work themselves out in their own unique way. You can regain ALIVENESS by allowing those thoughts, circumstances and feelings to be there, by letting go of your judgment about yourself that went with them, and by SURRENDERING to THE WAY IT IS. JUST BE IN THE FLOW.

Then create and CHOOSE as happening NOW a picture of what you really WANT to happen. Literally say to yourself: "I CHOOSE to have this turn out favorably!" Mock-up a picture of what that looks like as having already happened. Choose, contemplate and rehearse THAT as HERE, NOW! Write out a present-tense affirmation of what you see yourself having, doing and being in THAT picture.

If you notice resistance to doing the above, acknowledge the resistance and let it be there. If there's resistance to acknowledging the resistance, just notice that and let it be, ad infinitum, until you experience yourself being bigger than the prompts operating in your mind.

There's nothing else to do! You don't have to "fix," "handle," "change" or "eliminate" the thoughts or feelings. Just tell the TRUTH about them and go with them. They'll clear up in the process of the nature of things to work themselves out. TRUST the UNIVERSE to do what it does. Let water run around and over the obstacles. Let NATURE take its course! CHOOSE to be HAPPY.

If you have difficulty trusting that your life will turn out, let go of needing it to turn out by noticing and acknowledg-

ing the miracle that it is. Notice how much bigger that miracle is than the circumstantial content of your life. Get back in touch with contributing to others—with that beautiful love and connection that goes with acknowledging your part in this AMAZING natural universe.

Just add your love, inspiration and celebration to this miracle we call human life. AMEN and HALLELUJAH!

25

Some Practical Techniques

Get in touch with the mindset you've already used to successfully create something, and use it as a model for creating what you want now.

THE PROCESS described in this chapter is the result of my realizing one day that I might discover some valuable techniques I could use more consciously in the present if I just looked at all the things I'd already done successfully in the past. What I saw was that there were several key technique aspects which, if more consciously focused, could greatly enhance my chance of success.

The process described in this chapter is designed to make you aware of the way you've already successfully focused your Creative Mechanism, so you can then instruct your Creative Mechanism to IMITATE that way of operating in finishing what you're working on now.

This process will also get you in touch with, and assist you to acknowledge, where your resistance is to having the success you're seeking. This gives your Creative Mechanism valuable information about where you're starting from on the path to where you want to be.

Pick some result you WANTED that you successfully created some time in your life, and write that here. (Take the first thought that comes to your mind, and keep it simple.)

I once successfully created: ______________________________

____

____

Using the right side of the worksheet on page 107, summarize that successful result in a one- or two-word title and insert that title in the blank space at the top of column 1 in the space marked (*A*). Ask your Creative Mechanism to tell you how focused you were when you created that result by evaluating each focus aspect on a scale of 1 to 10, 10 being the highest.

How focused were you with respect to each of the ten technique aspects listed on the left side of page 107? Take the first number on a scale of 1 to 10 that comes to mind. Insert the number you get for each aspect in the respective blank opposite that aspect in the column headed *1*.

Now, pick some result you have WANTED but so far have been unsuccessful in creating and write that WANT here. (Again, take the first thought that comes to your mind.)

I want to: ____

____

____

Summarize this want into a one- or two-word title and insert that title in the blank space marked (*B*) at the head of column *2*. Make a similar evaluation of how focused you've been concerning each of the focus aspects with respect to creating this result.

Add up and total the two columns. Compare the point values in the two columns and their totals. The difference between the two totals gives you some indication of your resistance factor.

Now notice those technique aspects with respect to which you got the lowest scores in column *2*—as to the thing you're working on now. That's where your resistance is. Ask yourself what the source of that resistance is, and notice the first thought you get. Keep asking yourself what the source is of each answer you get, until you feel you've hit the truth and feel the significance lighten. Remember, you don't have to fix, handle or eliminate what you notice. Just acknowledge it, and you're free of its effect, while at the same time giving your Creative Mechanism necessary data about where you've been operating up to now. (See pages 108 and 109 for a sample of how I did this process with respect to throwing candies into a paper bag—Column 1—compared to getting a prior draft of this book finished—Column 2.)

Now, mock-up what it would "LOOK, SOUND, FEEL AND SMELL LIKE" if you operated with respect to the second WANT the way you operated with respect to the first WANT. IMAGINE WHAT IT WOULD BE LIKE. CONSIDER EACH FOCUS ASPECT. LITERALLY CREATE A PICTURE OF WHAT THAT WOULD LOOK, SOUND, FEEL AND SMELL LIKE, AND REHEARSE THAT. CONGRATULATIONS! NOW, JUST RELAX AND BE OPEN TO HAVING SOME MIRACLES!

CREATIVITY AWARENESS AND REFOCUSING GAME

	1 **First Want**	2 **Second Want**
	(A)________	**(B)**________
FOCUS ASPECTS		
1. INTENTION	________	________
2. EXPECTATION OF SUCCESS	________	________
3. VIVIDNESS OF PICTURE	________	________
4. RELAXED, TRUSTING OF SELF/UNIVERSE TO PRODUCE IT	________	________
5. EXPERIENCE OF "FUN" IN THE PROCESS	________	________
6. WILLINGNESS/WORTHINESS TO HAVE IT	________	________
7. RIGHT NOW/SOMEDAY	________	________
8. DAILY CHOICES IN ALIGNMENT WITH DESIRED RESULT	________	________
9. ACTUAL BEHAVIOR IN ALIGNMENT WITH DESIRED RESULT	________	________
10. OVERALL INTEGRITY IN LIFE —CREATIVE MECHANISM FREE OF UNFINISHED BUSINESS	________	________
TOTALS	________	________

CREATIVITY AWARENESS AND REFOCUSING GAME

Focus Aspects	1 First Want (A) Candies in Bag	2 Second Want (B) Book Finished
1. Intention	9	10
2. Expectation of Success	9	9
3. Vividness of Picture	9½	7
4. Relaxed, Trusting of Self/Universe to Produce It	8	7
5. Experience of "Fun" in the Process	9	8
6. Willingness/Worthiness to Have It	9	7
7. Right Now/Someday	10	7
8. Daily Choices in Alignment with Desired Result	9	6
9. Actual Behavior in Alignment with Desired Result	9	7
10. Overall Integrity in Life—Creative Mechanism Free of Unfinished Business	8	8
Totals	89½	75

The lowest value I got in column *2* was the "6" with respect to "Daily Choices in Alignment with Desired Result."

I then asked myself the following questions in writing and got the following answers:

Q: What is the source of my resistance to making the daily choices necessary to get my book finished?

A: The thought that I don't know what to do or how to do it.

Q: What is the source of that thought?

A: That I might fail.

Q: What is the source of that thought?

A: The belief that I would look foolish if I fail.

Q: What is the source of that belief?

A: The belief that making mistakes makes you a bad person.

Q: What is the source of that belief?

A: My childhood experience with the adults in my life to the effect that I was wrong if I made a mistake or did not do something perfectly.

(Within one week of doing the above process at dinner one Saturday night, the rewrite of my book was complete.)

26

The Natural State Is "Child"

There's no such thing as an "adult"—we're all children, forever. Let the "child" in you come out.

SEVERAL YEARS ago, when I first had the opportunity to address a high-school class, I asked myself what it was that I knew then (I was 51) that I wished I'd known when I was 18. Somewhat to my surprise, the first thought I got was not about the pearls of wisdom I'd learned in the various trainings I'd done. Rather, it was that I wanted these kids to know that we're all always children at heart, and that there's no such thing as an "adult."

I realized that I was 51 years old, and that I'd not yet achieved "adulthood" in my own eyes. It seemed as though in looking for the "adult" I was supposed to be, I'd been chasing the proverbial carrot on a stick that would always be just out of my reach.

When I looked around at the other people in my life's experience, I became convinced that there's no such thing as an "adult" anywhere. What I saw was only a bunch of "children" who'd been taught to "cool it"—to not be visionary, outrageous, off-the-wall, going for it, spontaneous, alive, growing, human beings—all in the name of so-called "adulthood."

It was about that same time that I started openly collecting and displaying little windup toys. I've yet to show them to a so-called "adult" who doesn't go wild over them. I give them with great success as birthday presents to my "adult" friends.

Interestingly, my dictionary defines the verb *adulterate* as: "To make inferior or impure by adding extraneous or improper ingredients."

We would all do well to remember the unfettered way in which very young children pursue life before the "good/bad" value system is laid on them. In my opinion, "child" is the true, natural state for all human beings—whatever the age. Wasn't it Jesus himself who said that to find the Kingdom of Heaven we need only be as little children?

Here's how I would define the child that we all are, forever:

A totally open, broad-minded, trusting, spontaneous, active, free-flowing, playful, imaginative, willing-to-be-outrageous, human being.

Ask yourself, "What would I be like today if that child that I was had been hugged and kissed and validated by my parents as much as I would like to have been?" Get as real and vivid a picture of yourself as that outrageous, enthusiastic and competent person you'd be today. Guess what? That wonderful, outrageous child that you were is still there, inside you, just waiting to be let out. CONTEMPLATE yourself as being that way and CHOOSE IT!

It's okay to come out and play.

27

Affirmations

Present-tense affirmations are powerful tools for focusing and pointing the Creative Mechanism at what you want.

FROM WHAT we've already said it should be fairly apparent how powerful positive affirmations can be in focusing the Creative Mechanism on what you WANT and creating it.

Although the ultimate vehicle for pointing the Creative Mechanism, in my opinion, is visualizing and rehearsing pictures of the result you want, expressing those pictures in words to the Creative Mechanism is extremely valuable, also. After all, computers communicate in language, and most if not all of the existing data in your Creative Mechanism is stored in the language you are accustomed to using.

Frankly, I don't know the exact roles language and visualization each play in effectively pointing your Creative Mechanism. What I do know is that *they both work*. You can identify and release old negative pictures and programming by noticing and paying attention to the words you hear yourself use to describe the choices you've made about what you want and expect to happen. Train yourself to notice when you express those choices in terms of what you want to fix, handle, break through or eliminate.

Get in the habit of recognizing these "pink elephants" as instances of your Creative Mechanism telling you about some negative programming under which you've been operating. You can easily transcend that by simply making the conscious choice to pursue that which is the pink elephant's positive opposite.

My work as a lawyer with written contracts has sharpened my awareness of the negative/positive implications of the words I hear myself and others use. I now notice very quickly when people are expressing themselves in terms of what they don't want, rather than what they *do* want. Whenever I notice myself using such a negative expression, I ask my Creative Mechanism to tell me what the "positive opposite" of that is. I then choose THAT, instead. I express THAT as an affirmation.

In the beginning, I had difficulty using affirmations that were stated in terms of "I am" something that wasn't yet literally true. The rational part of my mind said that such a statement is literally a lie. I found, instead, that I got a more effective present experience of the thing affirmed if I couched the affirmation in terms of my "EXPERIENCING" what it was I was affirming.

Below are some affirmations I found very effective. Write some or all of them, or some of your own, in your own handwriting as often as possible. According to John G. Kappas, in *Success Is Not an Accident*, handwriting in script is the most effective direction to the subconscious. (John also has a very effective format for directing the subconscious and acknowledging your successes in his "Mental Bank Concept.")

As you read or write each affirmation, momentarily mock-up experiencing the present existence of what that affirmation represents and just acknowledge any resistance or difficulty you have doing that. And remember that it is essential that you express and experience what you want as existing here in present time. As we saw in Chapter 8 (" 'Rev' Your Engine"), if you visualize in terms of "someday" having what you want, that's exactly when you'll get it. That approach turns what you want into the carrot on a stick tied to your back—always the length of that "someday" stick into the future. See and affirm yourself as having what you want NOW! (See Figures 10*a* and 10*b*.)

It would be valuable also to ask yourself what the "source" is of any resistance you notice in creating a present experience of the affirmation, and just acknowledge and let go of that resistance.

Figure 10*a*. Have the Carrot Be Here Now

Figure 10*b*. Imagine Yourself Being the Carrot You Want to Be!

SAMPLE POSITIVE PRESENT-EXPERIENCE AFFIRMATIONS

1. I experience myself easily and consistently having "fun" in everything I do.
2. I experience myself joyously and easily taking care of my body and health.
3. I experience myself joyously, easily and effectively surrendering to the "FLOW" of all things in this universe.
4. I experience myself joyously, easily and consistently inspiring the world with my love, wisdom and music.
5. I experience myself joyously, easily and consistently practicing mastery of life.
6. I experience myself joyously, easily and effectively being in this moment as "this is it."
7. I experience myself joyously, easily and miraculously experiencing my okayness, just the way I am right now.
8. I experience myself easily, enthusiastically and joyfully participating fully in life, with confidence and self-esteem.
9. I experience myself joyously, easily and effectively relaxing at all times and under all circumstances.
10. I experience myself joyously, easily and consistently handling all situations intuitively and effectively.
11. I experience myself joyously, easily and consistently trusting myself and my instincts under all circumstances.
12. I experience myself joyously, easily and consistently expecting only good things to happen to and around me.
13. I experience myself joyously, easily and effectively trusting myself and the universe to turn out for the highest good of myself and everyone around me.

14. I experience myself joyously, easily and effectively loving everything that I am, do and have.

15. I experience myself joyously, easily and effectively loving everything that I touch and that touches me.

16. I experience myself joyously, easily and consistently acknowledging my own knowledge, experience, worth and ability.

17. I experience myself joyously, easily and consistently loving and being loved.

18. I experience myself joyously, easily and miraculouly choosing, creating, and receiving what I WANT.

19. I experience myself joyously and easily receiving from the Source all the energy, inspiration and miracles I need and want.

I have found that the knowledge and experience of my Creative Mechanism, and how it works, has been the key to my being willing and able to practice positive, present-tense visualization techniques. Like everything else in life, it took some practice. If you are one of those persons like I was at first who has difficulty trusting the Creative Mechanism enough to use a really present-tense format, add the phrase "more and more each day" to the end of each affirmation. That's the way I had to do it until I had enough experience of the power of my Creative Mechanism to really trust it. Eventually, I even got to where I could give up the "I experience" form, and trust my Creative Mechanism to express my affirmations in the pure form: "I am. . . ."

I recommend also that you create your own affirmations by merely asking your Creative Mechanism what the affirmation is that you should use, given the particular result you want to achieve. Watch out for "what you don't want" formats, however. Those pull in the old "pink elephant" phenomenon. Express your affirmations only in positive terms. If your first expression comes out something like "to experience life without fear," acknowledge your former negative orientation and rephrase it into something like "to experience life with confidence and courage," etc.

If you're a smoker trying to quit, instead of saying "I experience myself as a nonsmoker," say something like "I breathe only clean, fresh air."

The following is an affirmation I got in answer to the question, "What is the picture I need to hold in order not to be so at the effect of the fear of failure and the judgment or reaction of others to me, my performance, or my good or bad circumstances?":

> *I am joyously, easily and effectively experiencing that the quality or worth of my life is simply a function of the degree to which I am true to myself in this present moment, and moment to moment.*
>
> *I am joyously, easily and effectively experiencing that the essence and nature of that to which I am true is simply the essence and nature of life itself—i.e. the miracle of just "being." Therefore I choose simply to do the best I can in this present moment, manifesting the person that I am right now with grace and ease. I am true first and foremost to the celebration of the miracle that is my life and the love that is in my heart, trusting myself and the universe to turn out.*
>
> *I easily experience myself behaving the way water behaves —free-flowing, allowing all obstacles and adversities to be what and where they are—yet, at all times true to my essential nature, intuitively KNOWING that I will find my true place FOR THE HIGHEST GOOD OF MYSELF AND OF ALL BEINGS AND THINGS IN THIS UNIVERSE.*

28

Intentional Listening

Communication is a single-path channel. Intentional listening clears the path so the other person can then hear you.

THE FLIP side, and probably more important side, of communicating your OWN truth is *listening to the other person.*

If each of us has an "investment" in our own point of view (that is, there is significance in the other person's agreeing with us), we program our Creative Mechanisms to believe that the success of that viewpoint has first priority. Then all the energy and flow is in the outward direction. However, there's only one path for communication between us. Information cannot flow on that path in both directions at the same time. So if you and I are both filling up that path with outflowing information, there's only the experience of bombarding each other, head-on, with facts and arguments, none of which ever really get heard.

The "pink elephant" phenomenon operates in communication, too. If you say something to me and I say "you're wrong," your natural impulse is to scan your data bank for more evidence and arguments to prove you're right. And we've made a "pink elephant" out of the differences between us.

The mind is a logic machine. Challenge its logic and it will automatically work to prove the correctness of its position.

For example, if you said to me, "It's your fault that our business is off this week," and I said, "You're wrong," the next thing we would both hear is you giving me a list of all the things I did wrong this week.

On the other hand, if you said, "It's your fault that our business is off this week," and I responded with "I understand how you feel. It sure looks like I caused us to lose business," I think you can see that you don't feel the same necessity to further convince me of the correctness of your first statement. If I then went on with something like "I sure would like your input on some ways to improve this week's performance," you might even be open to working with me, because you don't have to keep proving the accuracy of your first statement.

Real communication seems to operate like shortwave radio. You have to, in effect, say "Roger, over," and stop talking, before you can hear what the other guy has to say.

Can you feel good enough about yourself to let go of your OWN position long enough to acknowledge the other person's?

I recently had a conversation about the principles contained in this book with a man I'd just met. The acknowledgment of the existence of the Creative Mechanism, trusting that machinery and the power to CHOOSE what he wanted, had unlocked his whole life. (This was someone who had at one time been an alcoholic and drug addict and who was still angry, bitter and struggling.) When I spoke to him a few days later, he was higher than a kite out of the discovery of the existence of his Creative Mechanism. He also acknowledged noticing that he was hearing other people for the first time in a long time. And his wife corroborated that he seemed to have time for her that he never used to have. Also, little things didn't seem to upset him like they used to.

When I asked him what it was that enabled him then to hear other people, his answer was quick and brief: "I FEEL BETTER ABOUT MYSELF NOW!"

Remember, too, it is a great gift to give someone the opportunity to express what they need to express and thereby discover themselves. There's also incredible value for the listener. In being there for someone else, the listener has to give up his or her attachment to his or her self. That can be very inspiring and uplifting for the listener. Remember the vacuum principle discussed in Chapter 21.

I've experimented, with excellent results, with this kind of deliberate or intentional listening as an effective technique for avoiding the creation of "pink elephants" and for creating effective communication. When I notice myself in an argument now, I remember to stop pressing my own point of view and deliberately restate the other person's position so that there can be no mistaking that I got and understood what he or she was trying to tell me.

Invariably there's a distinct shift in the hitherto adversarial nature of the conversation, and some kind of miraculous resolution takes place. And this very often happens without my having any sense of really having to press my own point of view. I don't have to give up my own point of view to acknowledge somebody else's. I just stop making a "pink elephant" out of our differences by saying something like, "Let me see if I understand your position" and restate it, or "What I'm hearing you say is" and fill in the blank. I then let the other guy talk. I never forget what I had to say, and I don't have to "agree" with what the other person is saying. I only acknowledge the fact that it's being said.

Suppose you were Mr. Gorbachev in your first meeting with President Bush. Consider your reaction to an opening by President Bush that lists all the Soviet civil-liberties violations and demands assurance of further changes in Soviet policy before the talks go any further. Compare that to an opening that goes something like, "Congratulations on your work with the glasnost and perestroika programs. Tell me about Soviet life. I want to understand your history, your point of view and your needs."

If you look, I think you can see that the first opening comes out of a basic mindset that we are adversaries, whereas, the second one comes from the basic assumption that we are on this planet together—let's find a way to solve our differences for the good of humankind.

Again, the pictures we hold of the overall context will determine the behavior that ensues. And conversely, the behavior will demonstrate the picture from which the behavior is sourced.

Need I say more?

29

You Only "See" if You "Look"

The essence of "looking" is communicating.

VERY OFTEN the obvious escapes us. That "YOU ONLY SEE IF YOU LOOK" is one of those obvious principles we often overlook.

What I mean is that literally you can only see what is in the direction of where you're looking. However, when we're talking about discovering and empowering ourselves, what I've noticed is that I only see who I am by what I see myself do and hear myself say, and the way the universe reacts to that. The way the universe reacts to me is a function of what I'm projecting in my interaction with it.

Also, what I hear myself saying to others is very often something I hadn't noticed before, but which I, myself, needed to hear.

So, for me, an important process or technique by which I discover my own truth is to communicate and/or act out what I see is true. Every new experience or opportunity to communicate poses the question, "What do I see is true for myself about that?" When I look into my experience to see what it is I would say or act out about the subject at hand, my Creative Mechanism scans all the relevant data in my experience and comes up with that moment's unique expression of what is so for me about that subject.

The more I write and speak about the ideas in this book, the more I see about them. I cannot begin to tell you of the many new ideas and expressions that have come to me in the course of writing this book.

I AM CONSTANTLY HEARING MYSELF TELLING OTHERS WHAT I NEED TO HEAR! I commend to you the simple process of seeking and expressing your own particular truth. I imagine that the Roman Forum must have been the kind of place where the great thinkers of the day met and bounced their truths off each other.

The world has grown only out of people having the courage to speak their truths. I can tell you for certain, my own life has expanded in geometric proportions since I started doing that. One of the greatest gifts you can give anyone is to be the "space" into which they can express themselves. It is only through expressing ourselves that we ask ourselves that question the answer to which is what we need to hear.

There have been times when I spoke out with great enthusiasm, only to hear that somebody else had a different idea. When I "looked" again at what the truth really was, I saw that I'd missed something and was enriched and served by having my oversight pointed out to me. You will make that kind of discovery only if you SPEAK UP!

More often than not, however, you'll be acknowledged for your courage and the inspiration you are to others. I can't begin to tell you of the countless acknowledgments I've received out of the sharing I've done of the principles in this book and by means of the letters I've written, several of which have been read over the air or published in the newspapaer. I even sent President Reagan a game of ball darts in December 1984, inviting him to envision friendship with the USSR, just the way he would envision getting "bull's-eyes" or the way he envisioned becoming President. I warned him that what the President of the USA said publicly tended to program the whole world for that result. I do not claim to be the sole cause of President Reagan's shift in attitude, but I did get a written Thank You from his personal secretary, and his attitude did change toward the USSR.

The world has been moved and evolved out of the voice of the "crazies" who had the courage to keep speaking the truth as they saw it until enough people stood by them to make it a reality. Then they were called "visionaries."

I'm told that in East Germany about ten years ago, a small group of people began meeting once a week in Leipzig to pray for freedom. Word of that got around and more people showed up each week, until just before the Berlin Wall came down there were in excess of 10,000 people meeting in the streets of Leipzig.

Former poet and current President Vaclav Havel of Czechoslovakia spent five years in prison for speaking out for democracy. Look how many people are standing next to him NOW.

I have particular personal satisfaction in knowing that I had the guts to play my banjo and sing peace and freedom songs to people in Moscow, Leningrad, Dresden and East Berlin. In May of 1989 I told a bunch of college students in Dresden to stand up for what they believed in. Who knows, maybe one of them was instrumental in what eventually happened there. I know in my heart that a piece of what's going on in the world today, and of that Berlin Wall, belongs to me.

30

Practice Makes Perfect

Remember, it takes *practice* to learn new skills and to create new things in your life.

EVEN THOUGH you may be impressed with what the Creative Mechanism can do for motor-skill types of things, like walking and gymnastics, you might still be skeptical about whether it can operate in other aspects of our creative lives. Does it work there too? The answer is a resounding YES!

Starting from our traditional belief that there is something we have to figure out how to do—i.e. think our way rationally through the process of creation—it's easy to see how we would be reluctant to trust this Creative Mechanism to operate automatically, by itself, without any conscious help in things like job or relationship. When I first looked at trusting it for creating something other than double somersaults, I was very skeptical, too. Then I started noticing little things in my life where my Creative Mechanism operated automatically, taking care of me and giving me just what I needed, just when I needed it. I found objects and papers I could not previously find. I remembered things I needed to do at work and at home. I found just the perfect way of expressing what I wanted to say in presentations and in writing, both at work and socially. In fact, I started experimenting with surrendering to my automatic Creative Mechanism every time I noticed myself struggling to decide or figure something out. When I remember to use it, the results are spectacular.

Start building your confidence in your Creative Mechanism by simply noticing the little stuff it's already doing for you, like remembering names or phone numbers, especially when you relax and stop pressing it. As you notice each time in your life that the automatic machinery of this Mechanism takes care of you, the more you will trust it on bigger stuff and be able to point it without adding machinery-jamming stress and significance to the process or result. Remember, however, that the Creative Mechanism is very human. If you are squeezing it by the throat with both hands, it probably will not be capable of much communication. Relaxing and letting go is what allows it to do its job.

Also, like any other learning experience, it is best to choose some "easy" stuff to experiment with at first, in order to exercise this muscle under circumstances that will be low-key and not full of stress and significance. Pick something to play with where you are able to really TRUST your Creative Mechanism. Remember, too, it won't work if you're thinking, "What if it doesn't work?" However, if you notice that's what you're doing, just acknowledge that you did that, and rechoose what you want, and it will still work.

"Stretching" is a good technique, also. By that I mean, when you get a taste of the Creative Mechanism on easy stuff, stretch it by choosing something more difficult, like throwing the candies into the bag from several feet farther away, as we did in Chapter 3. Your mind may initially think that you will not be as effective from that distance as you were from up close. You should start up close, so you get a sense of accomplishment at first. When you "stretch" yourself, however, just "play" with it. Then go back to the closer distance and you'll find that it seems easier than it did before. You'll be more relaxed and more at reflex at that first distance after having "stretched" yourself. Remember, however, to always keep the "stretching" light and playful. Just hold it as a *game*.

Creating new things in your life is a trial-and-error, "zig zag" kind of process. It takes repetitive contemplation and rehearsal of the present existence of what you want, in order to record over the old tapes, especially when the old pattern comes to mind. Whatever you can do to remind yourself to stay in touch with what you said you WANTED is valuable, as long as you hold it in a way that allows the Creative Mechanism to take care of the "doingness."

Putting pictures and reminders of what you want on the wall or mirror is one way to communicate to your Creative Mechanism that you mean business. I've found, however, that things on the wall or mirror soon become just part of the wall or mirror, and that I need more than that to stay in focus.

The best thing you can do is to surround yourself with people who are in touch with this phenomenon and who are willing to support you in your process by reminding you of how wonderful you really are—people who will act as both space and mirror for you. Ask them to give you space by deliberate listening as described in the previous chapter, and to be your mirror by gently reminding you to look at the truth about where you are, where you want to be, and whether that includes "NOW" or not.

Your Creative Mechanism notices every time you say or do something, in terms of whether it is logically consistent or inconsistent with what you said you wanted. Get in the habit of—that is, *practice*—being more conscious from moment to moment of where you're pointing that machinery. Reread the material in this book and discuss these principles with others. That's a very powerful way to reinforce your intuitive trust of your Creative Mechanism.

I invariably hear myself telling others what I need to hear. And I gain new and wonderful insights in the process of asking myself what I'd say about a particular principle or application of it. This whole book is the product of just that kind of process. Remember, "You only see if you look." And "IF NOT NOW, WHEN?"

I also recommend that you write the following statements (filling in the blanks) as often as possible, preferably at night just before sleep:

1. *My purpose in life is* ________________________________

   ____

   (If you have difficulty identifying your true purpose, try asking yourself "What lesson am I here to learn in this lifetime?")

2. *What I want is* ________________________________

   ____

   (Describe the image of yourself having or doing whatever it is you want.)

3. *I experience myself projecting that image into the universe NOW, and experience the universe demanding my* _____

   ____

   (Fill in a description of what you want to have or do.)

4. *Things that I did, said, or happened today that were in alignment with what I said I wanted are:* ____________

   ____

   ____

   (Make a list of things that are evidence to your Creative Mechanism that you and/or the universe are in alignment with what you said you wanted. They don't have to be big things. If you have difficulty with these questions, ask yourself whether you really want what you said, and, if so, what the source of the resistance is. Either rechoose what you want, or CHOOSE something else.)

Remember, your Creative Mechanism gains strength from use. Just like your muscles, the more you use them, the stronger they get.

In recent years I've gotten involved with international Dixieland music, which I see as a powerful vehicle for demonstrating how we are really all the same. I asked a base player from an East Berlin band how people who play string instruments like violin, cello and base know where to put their fingers. (I play banjo, which has "frets" or bars that help me know where to put my fingers.) Hans' simple answer, with a great big smile, was "PRACTICE." And I've heard that other virtuosos say the same thing.

For example, a woman once approached world-famous violinist Fritz Kreisler after one of his performances with the comment, "I'd give my life to be able to play like that." Mr. Kreisler promptly replied, "Madam, I did." So you have to be willing to pay the price, in terms of practicing. But remember, success is not a function of the significance of the circumstantial things you accomplish. Success is a function of whether you are participating fully. If you are, you will have your share of traditional "success," because the universe will put you where what you're manifesting fits, à la Chapter 17.

There is no greater example of that, for my money, than the success achieved by Coach John Wooden of UCLA Basketball fame. As we mentioned in Chapter 21, Coach Wooden achieved 10 national championships in 12 years only after he learned to relax. I recently attended a ceremony in which the jerseys of UCLA greats Kareem Abdul-Jabbar and Bill Walton were retired. Bill Walton, in particular, acknowledged Coach Wooden's credo as a key ingredient to Bill's success in basketball:

> *Success is peace of mind, which is a direct result of self-satisfaction in knowing you did your best to become the best that you are capable of becoming.*

31

Are You Open to Miracles?

Miracles can only appear if you are open to having them and willing to take advantage of the opportunities they present.

I WANT to close this discourse with some of my favorite stories.

The first is a story of how Moses and Jesus played golf one day.

Jesus was the first to tee off. He took a mighty swing befitting his stature, but hooked the ball over the trees into the next fairway. (Moses began to anticipate an easy match.) However, as the ball came to a stop, a very large gopher ran up to it, picked the ball up in its mouth, and started to run away. (By now Moses is chuckling to himself.) When the gopher had gone about fifteen feet, a large eagle swooped down and clutched the gopher up in its claws. Gopher, ball, and all in its grasp, the eagle flew towards the mountains in the distance. (Moses is now rolling on the ground in hysterics.)

As it happened, the course the eagle was flying took it directly over the first green. Just at that moment, a bolt of lightning struck the eagle. The shock from the lightning caused the eagle to let go of the gopher, and the gopher to let go of the ball. You guessed it. The ball fell directly into the cup of the first green.

Moses turned to Jesus in disgust and said, "All right, do you wanna screw around, or do you wanna play golf?"

I used to tell that story thinking that Jesus was wrong for playing the game that way, and it wasn't because I was Jewish. It was because I believed that unless we adhere to the old way of doing things, the result doesn't count. The truth is, that the ball could have gotten in the hole the way I described it, via a gopher and lightning-struck eagle. Improbable, but possible.

I saw this even more clearly in throwing candies into the bag, when I noticed that I didn't count as successful responses the ones that bounced off the floor into the bag. If the result I was trying to create was to get the candy into the bag, why didn't I count the ones that bounced off the floor? I saw that what had really happened was that my Creative Mechanism (that had not been given any instructions as to "how" to get the candy into the bag) had simply guided my hand to throw the candy in a way that involved its bouncing off the floor into the bag.

By defining our goals in terms of persons, places or means we already know, we are limiting our expectations to only those persons, places and means with which we are already familiar. How incredible it would be to operate in life without all the limiting beliefs about how and from where things can happen! Free up your Creative Mechanism so it can draw upon all the infinite possibilities out there. Miracles are really only occurrences the cause of which we didn't see or understand. Be open to new, wonderful and previously unseen solutions and answers, and one might just fall out of the sky into your lap!

A great way to do that is to just let go of the names of known persons, places or means with which your old beliefs identify the result you want, and simply DEFINE what you WANT in terms of the QUALITY OF LIFE that represents. Defining your goal in terms of its QUALITIES makes it possible for your Creative Mechanism to draw upon the INFINITE universe as the source of the desired result. You'd better then be ready for some miracles!

The second story is about a very religious man who lived in an area that was susceptable to severe flooding when it rained. One winter there was a very severe storm forecast for this area, and all of its residents were informed they'd be evacuated by truck the next morning. When the truck came, our friend waved it on, saying that he trusted that God would take care of him.

As predicted, the storm raged on for four more days and the water level rose to his windowsills. At that time someone came by in a rowboat and offered to take him to safety. But our friend, who was now walking around in hip boots, stood fast in his faith that God would take care of him, even though the forecast was for a flood level that would totally inundate his house. He waved the boat away.

After four more days, the water level was at the roof, and our friend was sitting on the roof. A helicopter came by and dropped him a rope ladder. But again, he waved them away, professing his trust that God would take care of him.

The rains continued, the water rose over the roof, and our friend was swept away and drowned.

Being as religious as he was, our friend naturally went to heaven. As he was passing through the pearly gates, he saw St. Peter and stopped to ask how come God did not save him. He thought that God would have looked after such a devout person as himself. St. Peter promptly replied: "My dear Mr. Smith, we sent you a truck, a rowboat and a helicopter. What more do you want?"

The point, of course, is that so-called "miracles" take earthly form when they get here. If you're waiting for one with wings or an engraved "direct from God" on it, you'll drown first.

Be alert to the opportunities the universe (which may include God, if you are of that persuasion) presents to you, and CHOOSE to PARTICIPATE in those things that are in alignment with the QUALITY OF LIFE you said you WANTED. THERE ARE NO ACCIDENTS!

A MIRACLE, after all, is nothing more than an event, the cause of which was unexpected according the laws of nature with which we are familiar. Just because we can't anticipate or explain the causal connection doesn't mean there isn't one.

Remember, although improbable, it's literally possible for the golf ball to have gotten in the hole via a gopher, picked up by an eagle, shocked by lightning.

32

Where's Your Head?

Literally and figuratively, wherever you put your head, your body will follow.

ANOTHER PRINCIPLE of gymnastics seems appropriate here: WHEREVER YOU PUT YOUR HEAD, YOUR BODY WILL FOLLOW. From where I sit, this is true figuratively as well as literally.

Whenever I think of this principle I'm reminded of skier Bill Johnson and the way he won the Downhill Race in the 1984 Winter Olympics. Bill was a virtual unknown in world skiing circles going in. Yet, even before the actual race, he had all the so-called world-class skiers talking to themselves about his self-confident demeanor. Johnson "knew" he was going to win the gold medal, and his every muscle twitch reflected it. In other words, where his head was, in the figurative sense, was that he was going to win the race.

During the race, Bill literally and physically put his head into the skier's tuck (head down and forward) and kept it there, no matter what the terrain or bumps he encountered. The other skiers lifted their heads, causing their bodies to uncoil and create wind resistance, when they encountered one particularly difficult bump in the course. The fraction-of-a-second difference that Bill picked up on that one bump gave him the victory. Literally and figuratively, where Bill's head was, and stayed, won that race.

Conscious CHOICE is what determines where your head is, so you might as well just keep CHOOSING what you WANT at every bump in the course. Don't worry about the "how." Just

CHOOSE the result you WANT. The Creative Mechanism will take care of the "how" if you trust it to. If you forget how to trust it to do that, just throw some more candies in the bag with your eyes closed.

The third of my favorite stories is about a family that had two twin-boy children about eight years old.

One twin was an eternal pessimist and the other was an extreme optimist. The parents had great difficulty relating to this extreme behavior and went to a psychologist for advice. The psychologist recommended that the parents put the pessimist in a room for 30 minutes with nothing but the world's greatest toys. This, he said, would surely give the boy a more pleasant outlook on life.

For the optimist, he said, put him for 30 minutes in a room that has nothing in it but horse manure, a foot deep, wall to wall. He guaranteed that this unpleasant experience would break the child's unwarranted optimism.

The parents felt that these suggestions were a little extreme, but being desperate, went forward with the experiment.

When the 30 minutes were up, they opened the door to the pessimist's room only to find that he had smashed every toy in the room and was sitting in the middle of the rubble, crying his eyes out. The parents closed the door in disgust.

They then opened the door to the optimist's room where, to their amazement, they found their child having the time of his life, repeatedly digging into the manure with both hands and throwing it into the air with glee and excitement. Rubbing their eyes in disbelief at this apparent insanity, they mustered the courage to ask what in heaven's name the child thought he was doing. To which the child replied with great joy, "WITH ALL THIS HORSE MANURE, THERE MUST BE A PONY UNDER HERE, SOMEPLACE!"

Which twin are you?

33

A Harmonious World

With all the technical wonders we have created on this planet, surely we have the collective ability to create the harmonious world we want.

I WAS sitting out on the patio of the Federal Building in Westwood, California, musing at the complexity of today's world and the remarkable ingenuity demonstrated by the human race in coming from rocks and caves to things like automobiles, 80- or 100-story glass buildings, telephones, television, space shuttles, etc. The irony of it all is that it could all go up in a mushroom cloud at any moment. It was hard for me to believe that we could be that stupid.

It occurred to me that if I were an alien visiting from another planet I would find our civilization more than a little strange. On the one hand, I would marvel at the adaptability and ingenuity that has been demonstrated by earth's homo sapiens in getting from its prehistoric origins, with rocks and caves, to space shuttles.

On the other hand, I would be somewhat bewildered, I think, at the ways, number of times, and repetitive patterns our species has developed for mutilating, injuring and destroying itself and its environment.

What a waste of talent to build space shuttles while allowing its society to continually experience chronic, and now potentially fatal, internal and environmental disease. How myopic I would think it was to have invested so little of that talent and ingenuity in the structure of the society or in the sustainability of its environment—on how that society's parts relate to and interact with each other and its surroundings.

Is it too late? I think not.

I asked my Creative Mechanism what the society would look like if our species had applied its full genius to that issue.

The answer I got was that the society would be characterized by honest and open communication and the balancing of needs and resources as one total worldwide unit. Perhaps the principles that characterize the functioning of the life forces of one healthy human body could act as a model here. There's no greater miracle on this planet than the phenomenon that is the human body. Maybe we could copy some operating principles from that organism which would work at the level of society as well.

There'd be an intricate but workable system of individual cells, supporting and fulfilling each other's needs through accurate, honest communication, monitored, collated, interpreted and processed by an exquisitely complex but effective computer system that matches up the resources with needs, and gets them there through a system of appropriate arteries and vessels.

There'd of course be only ONE overall system for the entire organism, although subsystems would abound, each having its own unique function that befitted its location, history, and talent. Most of all, there'd have to be a healthy, holistic master program that was characterized by its positive, self-respecting and environment-respecting attitude. The system would take care of itself by imbibing only things that are nourishing to its continued existence. It would get plenty of exercise in the form of cooperative efforts of all of its parts to solve interactive and survival problems and explore space, and it would get adequate rest in the form of cultural and artistic exchanges, especially the sharing of things like music. It would play and have fun together. It would take care of itself and its surroundings as a whole.

I don't know about you, but that doesn't sound so far-fetched to me. Isn't it interesting that the technological aspects of that picture are now available in the form of the electronic computers and communication equipment and jet-propelled airplanes, etc. All we have to do is use them constructively by pointing them AT WHAT WE WANT. It is my experience that we are on that positive (albeit zig zag) course and just haven't fully awakened to it yet. A few more conscious CHOICES of the positive at this point will put us over the top.

I, FOR ONE, CHOOSE TO HOLD POSITIVE PICTURES IN MY MIND WITH RESPECT TO THE WORLD SITUATION. I'M GIVING MY HEART AND SOUL TO THE PICTURE OF A WORLD AT PEACE WITH DIGNITY AND ABUNDANCE FOR ALL, NO MATTER HOW OFF-THE-WALL (OR UNDER THE HORSE MANURE) THAT MAY SEEM TO SOME PEOPLE RIGHT NOW. I KNOW IN MY HEART THAT THE SOLUTIONS WILL MAKE THEMSELVES KNOWN IF WE ARE OPEN TO RECEIVING THEM, AND THAT, IF WE "REV" OUR COLLECTIVE ENGINES TOWARD THE POSITIVE, WE WILL FIND WAYS TO CREATE IT.

As Richard Bach so beautifully put it in *Illusions*: "Argue for your limitations, and they are yours."

As Buckminster Fuller said in *Operating Manual for Spaceship Earth*:

To disclose to you your own vanity of reflexing, I remind you quickly that none of you is consciously routing the fish and potato you ate for lunch into this and that specific gland to make hair, skin, or anything like that. None of you are aware of how you came to grow from 7 pounds to 70 pounds and then to l70 pounds, and so forth. All of this is automated, and always has been. There is a great deal that is automated regarding our total salvation on Earth, and I would like to get in that frame of mind right now in order to be useful in the short time we have.

I trust that if you've gotten this far in the book, you've tasted enough of the Creative Mechanism you have to know that we don't have to see the "how to do it" in advance of CHOOSING THE POSITIVE RESULTS WE WANT in this world. I therefore hope that you'll join me in letting go of haranguing the evidence of how bad it's been up to now, and envision the world the way we want it to be. History repeats itself mainly because we keep looking for and giving lip service to evidence that supports our judgments about how "bad" the past has been. Our only real chance for success is to envison what we WANT, and to have the courage to speak out for that as a present reality.

I've been wearing my EGBOK button almost every day for many years. I even wear it in important business meetings. When people ask me what it means and I tell them, "Everything's Gonna Be Okay," they invariably agree.

However, the real truth about saying that "it's GONNA be okay" is that you're telling your Creative Mechanism that "SOMEDAY in the future you'll get what you want." Remember, the Creative Mechanism takes what you tell it very literally. So, in order not to keep that person indefinitely pointed into the future and never experiencing present satisfaction in life, I usually add that "it's gonna be okay" is not really the whole truth. "EVERYTHING *IS* OKAY" is what makes it so. After a moment's pause to reflect, they invariably agree. You see, in the cosmic sense that is really so. Things are what they are, and it's only our learned value judgments that make "pink elephants" out of them.

I meet a lot of wonderful people through wearing my EGBOK button, and at the same time reinforce my and their experience of the fact that the world IS actually turning out. There are a lot more people out there willing to be that positive than you might think. They just need to be reminded. Please join me in that pursuit.

If I were to put my feeling about the world in a present-tense affirmation, it would go something like this:

I EXPERIENCE THIS CIVILIZATION ON EARTH AS ONE FAMILY, TRULY AT PEACE, WITH DIGNITY, MUTUAL RESPECT, LOVE AND ABUNDANCE FOR ALL.

Thank you for allowing me to share my truths with you.

APPENDIX
Questions and Answers Used to Create This Book

Q: *What is it I want to accomplish in writing this book?*

A: [Had two false starts to answers that did not feel right and was experiencing difficulty getting a clean answer. I acknowledged this resistance to myself, and asked the question again.]

A: (1) To contribute inspiration to the understanding and acceptance in the world of the principles involved in the Creative Mechanism that exists in each and every human being, to the end that individuals will dare to choose and empower their own visions, and all the countries of the world will dare to declare the vision of a world truly at peace with freedom, dignity and abundance for all humankind.

(2) To have my own life be a demonstration of the power of the Creative Mechanism about which I speak. (One of my visions is to be rich and famous as a teacher, trainer, writer, lecturer and counselor in the power of the Creative Mechanism in each of us and to have that be my vocation rather than my avocation.)

Q: *What is the key notion I want to get across?*

A: [The answer I got was that I had not asked the right question and so I asked myself what was the proper question for getting the answer I wanted.]

Q: *What is the key question in the life of almost every human being, organization or country in the world today?*

A: "How do I create what I want to have in my circumstances that I don't yet have?"

Q: *What is the key notion that most people, organizations and countries are overlooking with respect to how they can create what they want?*

A: That each human being has an automatic guidance system (the "Creative Mechanism") that will handle the "how" if given reasonably clear instructions ("visions") of the desired result.

Q: *What is the importance of the recognition, acknowledgment and empowerment of that mechanism?*

A: Accepting the existence of the Creative Mechanism makes it possible to postulate visions of results, the means for the production of which are not yet apparent or at hand—i.e. to trust oneself, others and the Universe, and give energy and support to the desired result instead of to doom and gloom.

Q: *What needs to be communicated so that people will readilly be in touch with the Creative Mechanism and be willing to trust it?*

A: (1) An explanation of the inverse dynamics of the mechanism.

(2) Examples of its everyday use.

(3) Explanation and examples of the power of focusing the mind: Aikido and Ralph Strauch's resisting-resistance demonstrations.

(4) Examples of people who have freed self of limiting beliefs: e.g. one-legged marathon runner, kids doing "wheelies," gymnastics, baseball hitters and pitchers,